THE BUREAUCRACY and THE LEGISLATIVE PROCESS

A Case Study of the Health Care Financing Administration

CHESTER A. ROBINSON

UNIVERSITY PRESS OF AMERICA

Lanham • New York • London

University Press of America®, Inc.
4720 Boston Way
Lanham, Maryland 20706

3 Henrietta Street
London WC2E 8LU England

Printed in the United States of America
British Cataloging in Publication Information Available

This book was written by Chester A. Robinson in his private capacity. No offical support or endorsement by the Health Care Financing Administration or the Department of Health and Human Services is intended or should be inferred.

Library of Congress Cataloging-in-Publication Data

Robinson, Chester A., 1950-
The bureaucracy and the legislative process : a case study of the Health Care Financing Administration / Chester A. Robinson.
p. cm.
Includes bibliographical references and index.
1. Medicare—Law and legislation.
2. Legislation—United States.
3. Executive power—United States.
4. United States. Health Care Financing Administration.
5. United States. Congress.
6. Bureaucracy—United States. I. Title.
KF3608.A4R63 1990
344.73'0226—dc20 [347.304226] 90–23445 CIP

ISBN 0–8191–8117–X (alk. paper)
ISBN 0–8191–8118–8 (pbk. : alk. paper)

The paper used in this publication meets the minimum requirements of American National Standard for Information Sciences—Permanence of Paper for Printed Library Materials, ANSI Z39.48–1984.

*In Inspiration for Andrew and Dallas
to Expand Beyond What You
Know You Can Be*

Acknowledgements

Regardless of how the title page reads, no author produces a book alone. There are many individuals I should thank who contributed to the successful completion of this book. While it is not possible to identify them all here, I sincerely appreciate their many contributions.

Equally important are colleagues, who keep you on your toes, support you, and if necessary, bring you back to reality. In this respect, special appreciation is due to Dr. Julianne Mahler and Dr. Timothy Conlan, of the Department of Public Affairs, George Mason University, Fairfax, Virginia. Many of the central ideas expressed in this book grew out of our collaborative efforts. They have also contributed their time, thought and insights far beyond any reasonable expectation. I am also grateful for their assistance in improving both the organization and coherence of my presentation.

Special thanks are due to the interviewees for the study—the career and political staffs at the Health Care Financing Administration (HCFA) and Congressional committee staffs. Without the frank and intelligent insights of these talented professionals, this book would not have been possible. I owe particular gratitude to Carleen Talley, of the Division of Legislative Services and Congressional Affairs, HCFA, for her openness and extensive cooperation in the collection of agency and congressional legislative documents used in this study.

Finally, thanks are due to my family, who put up with prolonged preoccupation with this book and irascibility. Responsibility for factual errors and normative excesses is my own.

—CHESTER A. ROBINSON
Columbia, Maryland

Contents

Foreword

The involvement of federal administrative agencies in the legislative process has grown enormously since the turn of the century. The role of agencies, such as the Health Care Financing Administration (HCFA), in formulating legislation has increased significantly in both scope and complexity. Dr. Robinson demonstrates the relative importance of the bureaucracy in the development of Medicare legislation, vis-a-vis the President and the Congress. He focuses on identifying patterns of behavior in the legislative process. He highlights what each organizational legislative actor does, when and how, in developing Medicare legislation. More important, Dr. Robinson investigates "why" and "what difference it makes."

Of course, an exact determination of the contributions of all the relevant actors in the legislative process, in general or on a particular piece of legislation is virtually impossible. The legislative process is too dynamic for such a determination. Nonetheless, by clarifying the often overlooked contributions of the bureaucracy, Dr. Robinson has made a significant contribution to our understanding of the basic rudiments in formulating legislation.

Dr. Robinson appropriately points out that the resources available to the bureaucracy puts it in a good position to make significant contributions to legislative development. Taking a generic look at enacted Medicare legislative initiatives and the inherent features of the bureaucracy, it becomes apparent that they have several complimentary features. In my experience as a HCFA Administrator, I found that the following list was a useful yardstick to help gauge the likely enactment of a legislative proposal:

- The legislative idea has sufficient "strength" to gain serious consideration. The proposal must be perceived as a benefit to the Medicare program or at a minimum, to do the program no harm.
- The proposal is legislatively "ripe". The most essential ele-

element here is that proposals must be fashioned to reflect current political thinking and needs. The legislative timing, receptivity of the Congress and the White House, and political sponsorship are also critical elements in determining ripeness.

- The proposal must offer some political value or be considered politically palatable.
- It must be well conceived analytically and be supported with verifiable data.
- Proposals designed to enhance administrative efficiency or produce program savings have a greater likelihood of enactment.

Because administrative agencies like HCFA have a focus on problem solving, it makes them intuitively able to furnish these necessary elements for successful legislation. HCFA has the staffing resources, the expertise, is imbued with a sense of mission and is organized in an efficient and coordinated fashion. Because of these resources and its vast information gathering capabilities, HCFA is placed in a good position for developing analytically well conceived legislative proposals.

Perhaps more importantly, HCFA's ongoing involvement in the legislative process allows it to recognize and seize opportunities to advance legislative initiatives at politically opportune times. The agency's close relationship with the White House and the Congress affords it with favorable circumstances to gauge their legislative needs, goals and moods.

As demonstrated in this book, these are the ingredients that the bureaucracy, by its nature, is well suited to supply to the legislative process. I know of no other book that identifies the contributions of the bureaucracy in such detail and successfully integrates the prevailing theories of the day with the reality of the bureaucratic experience.

Carolyne K. Davis, Ph.D.
Administrator,
Health Care Financing Administration
1981–1985

Preface

In the daily news media we hear a great deal about the advancement of "new legislative proposals." However, what is noticeably absent is any substantive discussion on how these proposals were brought into being. Working as a legislative analyst in the Health Care Financing Administration, this omission was particularly apparent to me. Early in my career I was convinced of the importance of expanding our knowledge of the development stage of the legislative process. It is vitally important to our understanding of any legislative initiative that we have an appreciation for its evolution before entering the highly focused political arena.

This book examines the relationships the President and the Congress have with the bureaucracy in formulating legislation. It questions some traditional perspectives on their respective roles as legislative policy makers. It is the result of research designed to demonstrate that civil servants participate in the legislative process in ways other than to faithfully implement the laws Congress has enacted. It demonstrates that civil servants participate in essentially all phases of the legislative process, particularly in the formulation of legislative recommendations. This is as much a function of the bureaucracy as implementing the laws enacted by the Congress.

Recognizing the distinction between the role that conventional wisdom dictates that civil servants should play and the role they in fact do play in the legislative process is of tremendous importance to our understanding of the legislative process. Only by questioning long standing assumptions about the respective roles of the President, the Congress and the bureaucracy in the development of legislative initiatives can we fill the void in our understanding of the actual legislative process. In this manner we can discern clear cut patterns in the formulation of legislative initiatives. Perhaps we can develop a theoretical "road map" for the generation of future legislative initiatives.

Such a road map could serve as guide for those who want to

initiate new legislative policies by preventing the misdirection of resources and pointing to paths that have led others to success. But the primary importance for those of us with a special interest in legislative policy formulation, is that it would fill the void in our understanding of what goes on in the little black box labeled "legislative initiation." In a democracy it is essential that information be available on how government works, how decisions are made, what forces impact on policy making, and how opinions, especially those from outside the government, affect the formulation of legislative initiatives.

In some form, we have all contributed to the ambiguity in the role of the bureaucracy in our legislative system. We have generally wanted civil servants to be neutral, yet we want them to be responsive to the political party in power. In this respect, I concur with Ezra Suleiman who points out that the most important contribution of studies like this is to help shift the focus of attention from the normative question of "the role civil servants ought to play in formulating legislation" to the behavioral one of "what influence do civil servants exert on the legislative process." This shift in emphasis has considerable implications for how we, as American citizens, perceive our governmental system.

CHAPTER I

Introduction

Few political issues are more fundamental to Public Administration than the question of the bureaucracy's role vis-a-vis the Congress and the President in governing our country. In the phrasing of Arthur M. Schlesinger and Alfred de Grazia, the first step to understanding the American governmental system is to recognize that the "Constitutional Convention created, not a government of separated powers, but . . . a government of separated institutions sharing powers."[1] When these powers are put together, they constitute the American governmental system.

The reading of any basic text in political science makes it abundantly clear that the President and the Congress are both intimately involved in the legislative process. Regrettably, the role of the bureaucracy in the legislative process is not as clear. That is a deficiency this book hopes to remedy.

The implicit assumption in this basic literature is that the bureaucracy is "considered a factor in legislative formulation, but more often than not, it is felt to be appropriately placed in the background." This is attributable to the generally accepted notion that the civil service is neutral in the legislative process, and is under the "control of both the President and the Congress."[2]

It is often overlooked that one of the ancillary tasks of administrative agencies is to recommend legislative proposals to the President and the Congress that reflect their operational experience as well as to formulate policy through administrative rule.[3] Because the bureaucracy does not participate directly in the enactment process, but provides recommendations and technical assistance, its contributions to the legislative process are often overlooked and poorly understood.

Part of the reason for this is that neither the role of the President, the Congress, nor the bureaucracy is monolithic. Legislative circumstances differ in the opportunities they provide in particular instances. Yet, it is apparent that each of these participants in the legislative process—bureaucrats, legislators and the President—bring different criteria and contributions to legislative development.[4]

In an effort to explore the role of the bureaucracy in a more complete and systematic fashion, this research describes the contributions of the Health Care Financing Administration (HCFA) to the Medicare legislative initiation process. We contend that HCFA participates actively in the development of legislation with the President and the Congress by helping them to diagnose public problems, assisting in the development of legislative recommendations in addition to providing them with Medicare program technical assistance.

In examining HCFA's role in the legislative initiation process, three different activities are examined to more accurately describe its contributions. These activities include: (1) assisting in the formulation of the President's legislative agenda, (2) consulting with the Congress on Medicare legislative proposals, and (3) serving as a "semi-independent" actor in the Medicare legislative initiation process.

These three activities performed by the agency permit us to isolate its role in the legislative process in a more precise manner. In this fashion, responsibility for Medicare legislative initiatives can be fixed more precisely. In the words of political scientist (now member of Congress), David E. Price, "the problem is not so much to ascertain whether Congress or the executive enjoys a general policy making preeminence as to understand exactly who does what."[5] The findings of this investigation will have general implications for HCFA's administrative role in the legislative initiation process and provide a bench mark for assessing the specific role other agencies play in the legislative process.

The Bureaucracy's Legislative Contributions Are Obscured

It is apparent to those who study government organizations—and particularly to those who work in them—that the role of the bureaucracy in the legislative process is not limited to situations where government agencies have been given formal authority to make rules implementing legislation that Congress has passed.

Civil servants in the Health Care Financing Administration (HCFA), as well as other federal administrative agencies, are in intimate contact with the everyday operations of their programs. This provides them with an excellent vantage point from which to see the need for new legislative initiatives. It is also evident that they are best able to determine the technical and administrative feasibility of legislative initiatives that are developed elsewhere, as well as those under active consideration by the Congress or the President.

The basic premise of this book is that HCFA and other federal administrative agencies typically become involved in the early stages of the legislative process because of their operational knowledge of programs, expertise and staffing resources. They become involved both formally and informally by providing inputs in the form of "technical assistance and recommendations" to the White House and Congress when legislation is being formulated.

Because the major portion of the agency's role in the legislative process is indirect, the extent of thesc "inputs" often goes undetected by scholars who do not have close familiarity with the bureaucracy. Moreover, the agency's involvement in the legislative process is frequently informal. That is, much of its activities and contributions in forming Medicare legislative initiatives are located beneath the surface of the formal enactment process. This subterranean system arose because the bureaucracy only has the ability to "advise" the President and the Congress on legislative matters. It offers support, recommendations, technical advice and professional assistance. HCFA does not have formal constitutional authority to participate directly in the legislative process.

Historians tell us that informal participation in the legislative process was the case for administrative agencies as early as the Jeffersonian period in American history. "Substantially all major legislation and much minor legislation," writes administrative historian Leonard White, "was based on administrative reports, giving facts and opinions for the guidance of Congress."[6]

More recently, Steven Kelman reemphasized this point, stating that "government agencies often bring to the attention of Congress and the White House problems that need examination." Kelman states that agencies routinely "provide specific proposals for dealing with them [problems], even proposing statutory language."[7]

Unfortunately, to explain the disparity between the bureaucracy's formal role and its actual role in the legislative process, students cannot turn readily to the current body of literature in Political Science and Public Administration for insights or inspiration. Students find themselves confronted with a myriad of theories and models that often overlook the informal role of the bureaucracy, or focus on broad societal or structural explanations of the legislative process. In an effort to provide direction for future legislative scholars, we evaluate which theoretical approaches best explain how staff in administrative agencies contribute to the development of legislation in actual practice.

Since essentially all federal agencies have staff involved in developing or evaluating legislative initiatives, it would be desirable to examine the nature and workings of one of them. This book does so through an exploratory study of the role of the Health Care Financing Administration (HCFA) in the development of Medicare legislation. In doing so, we can assess the accuracy of several theoretical assumptions of conventional wisdom that explain bureaucratic influence on the development of legislative initiatives.

The Complexity of Initiating Legislation

As a reference point for exploring the role of the Health Care Financing Administration (HCFA) in legislative policy initiation, a fundamental question is posed:

> At the agency level, who is involved, and to what extent, in the development of Medicare legislative initiatives?

Using this fundamental question as our point of inquiry, we can probe more deeply to determine answers to more precise questions, such as "what agency officials would be involved in developing legislation for a Medicare catastrophic health insurance plan?—a long-term care program?—or a Medicare program to cover preventive health services?" It is likely that specific people can be identified. Indeed, other authors, such as Charles Jones, contend that "it is quite probable that a legislative formulation system with rather established processes exists to act upon such issues."[8]

At the national level of legislative formulation, it is possible to identify various groups, even specific individuals, from which

Medicare legislative policy initiatives are drawn. It is also possible to make some general observations about the roles these groups and individuals play in initiating Medicare legislation. First, legislators and their staffs are involved in Medicare legislative initiation. A second major source of Medicare legislative initiatives is the Executive Branch—both appointed and career civil servants. Another major source for initiatives is the private sphere—including a variety of specific interest groups.[9]

These are the actors in the legislative process that are most evident. However, the more difficult and complex task in examining how Medicare legislative policies are initiated is to discern:

(1) Who is involved in which significant set of activities in the Medicare legislative initiation process? Is HCFA a primary initiator of Medicare legislation or does it merely react to initiatives developed elsewhere?

(2) What type of interaction does HCFA have with the White House and Congress in the development of Medicare legislative initiatives?

(3) What particular resources do agency staff bring to the legislative policy initiation process?

(4) What are the specific Medicare legislative outputs of the agency? For example, does it produce specific legislative proposals? If so, in what form? How are agency reactions to congressional initiatives relayed to the Congress?

When these types of questions are posed, it becomes clear that the role of federal administrative agencies in formulating legislative initiatives is not clearly defined in the existing body of literature. There is no "neat division of functions" among the various actors involved in legislative initiation.

This can be illustrated by some concrete cases highlighting HCFA's role in the complex process of initiating Medicare legislation.

Case #1

In October 1984, a mid-level civil servant at the Health Care Financing Administration (HCFA) receives an assignment from his supervisor to respond to a letter to the President. The writer is a single school teacher in California who has recently retired.

She has discovered that her State medical insurance coverage will not be available to her in retirement. In addition, because she has not worked under the Social Security system, she is not eligible for Medicare benefits.

Recognizing that the teacher's situation is not unusual, the civil servant becomes an advocate within the agency for a change in the Medicare statute. He makes a two-fold argument that if State and local governments were required to provide Medicare protection to their employees the same as private employers, it would: (1) increase revenues to the financially troubled Medicare trust funds, and (2) provide Medicare health insurance protection to individuals in situations like the retired California school teacher.

He is successful in persuading officials in his agency on the merits of his arguments. A legislative proposal is developed and submitted to the Executive Office of Management and Budget. It is accepted and included in the President's legislative program and transmitted to the Congress. After a series of Congressional hearings, on July 31, 1985 the House Committee on Ways and Means announces that it has reported legislation establishing new policies which require the payment of the Medicare tax by State and local governments for their employees. This legislation was subsequently enacted into law.

The point of this case is to demonstrate that civil servants are often the first to become aware of problems, program inadequacies and opportunities for legislative initiatives. Second, in order to formulate legislative initiatives, the presence of an effective process that permits the transmission of expert input into the legislative process is needed. In this way, the influence of the agency manifests itself in the development of legislation in the Executive Branch as well as the Congress.

Case #2

Speaking at a forum on the Presidency at the University of Texas, Wilbur Cohen, former Secretary of the Department of Health, Education and Welfare, stated that it is commonly known that both Presidents Kennedy and Johnson proposed Medicare. While they deserved a great deal of credit for advocating it, neither thought it up. Cohen said that Medicare was introduced in Congress in 1951; however, from 1951 to 1957, nobody of any political importance endorsed it. Nothing happened until 1960 when Kennedy supported it. It was defeated in 1960. It was defeated again in 1961, 1962 and 1964. Finally, President Johnson said, "This is a major part of my legislative program, and I'm going to put my imprimatur on it." After Johnson won a landslide victory in 1964, Wilbur Mills, who was the chairman of the powerful House Ways and Means Committee, changed his views on Medicare because Lyndon Johnson had the votes in the Congress to pass it over his objections and the Medicare law was enacted in 1965.[10]

The essential lesson here is that Congressional action on legislative initiatives can be accelerated as a direct result of Presidential endorsement and electoral landslides. Given these political factors, what are the implications for the bureaucracy's participation in the legislative process? Does an administering agency, such as HCFA, have increased discretion in formulating legislative initiatives when both the White House and the Congress are controlled by the same political party, or is legislative policy essentially set by the White House and the Congress?

Conversations with staff of the then Medicare Bureau of the Social Security Administration, who participated in the development of the original Medicare legislation in 1965, overwhelmingly indicate that the agency's role was considerably enhanced in the legislative process. They indicate that while the Congress and the White House set the basic legislative framework for the Medicare program, its technical aspects and administrative mechanisms were essentially designed by a relatively small staff of agency experts. Agency staff, working informally in conjunction with White House and Congressional committee staffs, formulated major parts of the Medicare program that were subsequently enacted into law. It would appear then that the agency's role in Medicare legislative initiation can be significantly enhanced as a result of a successful political campaign.

Case #3

On January 31, 1985, Senator David Durenberger, Chairman of the Senate Finance's Subcommittee on Health introduced three bills to impose higher Medicare costs on individuals who smoke. These bills would have also provided Medicare coverage for certain preventive health measures. In his intro-

> ductory remarks Senator Durenberger stated that health plan buyers should be financially encouraged to reduce their risk of illness and made to contribute more if they choose to increase their sick care consumption risk through smoking or other obviously dangerous habits.
>
> Durenberger's actions were not only spurred by the zeal of his personal commitment to stop smoking, but also by Surgeon General's reports beginning in the 1960's, indicating that smokers are at greater risk of disability and fatal illness than nonsmokers. He was also spurred by private health and life insurance companies who were already taking the lead in rewarding those who chose to avoid smoking. As the noted gerontologist, Ann Somers has argued, "The time has passed when the American tax payer can pay for full coverage of health benefits to the victims of known self-destructive behavior without asking for an additional contribution from them."
>
> Despite these movements in both the private and public sectors, no action was taken on these bills. It was not until 2 years later with the enactment of the Omnibus Budget Reconciliation Act (Public Law 100-203) on December 22, 1987 that Senator Durenberger was successful in getting a more modest version of the legislative directive passed. This legislation directed HCFA to conduct a major study to determine the extent of the problem and how best to incorporate such a financing mechanism into the Medicare program.[11]

In this case we observe that an individual legislator and his/her staff can be instrumental in getting items placed on the congressional legislative agenda and enacted into law. Many individual legislators have been recognized as the champion of certain pieces of social legislation or "pork barrel" legislation that favors a particular constituency.

In this case, however, it should be noted that because HCFA is responsible for conducting the study, the agency will be the primary decision-maker in determining its design, parameters, and in evaluating the study's results. This gives HCFA considerable discretion in defining the extent of the problem and in determining how best to incorporate such a financing mechanism into the Medicare program. Since the Congress will probably rely heavily on the agency's study findings in any subsequent legislative initiative, HCFA will likely have a significant role in determining the substance of the legislative initiative; if indeed, the agency does not draft the legislative initiative.

Although anecdotal and incomplete, these three cases suggest the importance and complexity of HCFA's participation in the formulation of Medicare legislation. They indicate that the agency's contributions include investigating and defining problems, researching and commenting on legislation, providing advice on alternative means of achieving goals and determining whether proposals are administratively feasible. They also show that we must avoid simplistic notions of constitutional separations of powers, and of presidential, congressional or bureaucratic dominance of legislative initiatives. Such notions are inadequate to explain the very complex process by which Medicare legislation, and perhaps other domestic legislation, is initiated in this country.

Why Study the Health Care Financing Administration?

This study used the Health Care Financing Administration (HCFA), an agency in the Department of Health and Human Services, as a laboratory to investigate the role of federal administrative agencies in the legislative process. In terms of both its budget and the number of people it serves, the Health Care Financing Administration is one of the largest enterprises, public or private, in the United States. In Fiscal Year 1990, HCFA will spend about $130 billion under the Medicare and Medicaid programs to provide for the health care needs of 53 million aged, poor, and disabled citizens in this country. Every day, about 800,000 Medicare and Medicaid beneficiaries see a physician; 300,000 receive care as hospital inpatients; and about 90,000 receive the services of nursing homes. In addition, thousands of other beneficiaries daily receive home health visits, drugs, health screening, kidney dialysis, or a wide range of other services.

The agency's basic mission is to ensure the timely and appropriate delivery of these services through effective administration of the Medicare and Medicaid programs. These programs are administered through a complicated set of relationships involving the private insurance industry, government institutions at the state and local level, and thousands of independent hospitals, physicians and other providers of health care services.

Despite the magnitude of its responsibilities, in terms of staff, HCFA is one of the smaller major agencies in the federal government with 5,000 employees. This staff must monitor 70,000 full-time employees of states and contractors as well as about 360,000 physicians, hospitals and other health care providers.

During the period covered by this study the Medicare program had a series of legislative changes enacted into law. Some of these changes, such as the Medicare Prospective Payment System, have had a dramatic impact on how medical care is delivered and financed throughout the nation. Others have been modest or technical in scope. The span of this study also includes periods with different political parties in control of the White House and the Congress, as well as periods of rapid program expansion and budgetary cutbacks.

As a major participant in formulating Medicare legislative initiatives, HCFA has the expertise, staffing resources and the technology necessary to perform substantive legislative analyses. The agency funds and conducts millions of dollars in research projects and data collection to support Medicare legislative policy decisions.

In his book, *Bureaucratic Policy Making,* Gerald S. Gryski strongly suggests that these resources are important elements in government policy making.[12] That is, having a battery of trained experts armed with technological knowledge about their particular programs is a necessary ingredient in the development of programmatically sound legislative initiatives. In this respect, Gryski supports the thesis in this book that legislation which effectively addresses complex programmatic problems simply cannot be formulated without the assistance of these experts and the availability of scientifically acquired data.

Another important reason for the use of HCFA as a prototype is that the agency is an active advocate for its legislative initiatives in both the Executive and Congressional health legislative arenas where political forces interact to mold legislative initiatives. Because the agency consults with both the Congress and the President in a formal, as well as an informal basis, it has ongoing access to the constitutional machinery that is necessary to place Medicare initiatives on the Nation's legislative agenda. So, in addition to substantive knowledge, a second essential legislative policy making element is present in HCFA that provides for the efficient transmission and utilization of expert input in the legislative process.

In sum, within the confines of its organizational structure, HCFA harbors the expertise and the elements necessary to advance its legislative proposals to the legislative arena. For these reasons, the agency offers fertile ground for an examination of the principles that guide decision makers in legislative initiation.

A Brief Overview of the Research

In examining how HCFA participates in the legislative process, three different roles were studied to more accurately describe the agency's contributions. These roles include examining HCFA's legislative activities as they relate to: (1) assisting in the formulation of the President's legislative agenda, (2) consulting with Congress on the impact of legislative proposals, and (3) serving as a "semi-independent" actor in initiating legislative proposals.

While this study employs a single research method (i.e., the case study), it does use multiple techniques or measures to collect and interpret data. Through the use of the multiple technique approach, greater levels of confidence in the study's findings can be developed than would have otherwise been possible had a single measure been used. Moreover, the use of multiple measures (or techniques) helps to elicit findings that may have otherwise gone unnoticed or underdeveloped.[13]

There are four major parts to the study's research design. The first involves a search for the origins of the Medicare provisions of the Omnibus Budget Reconciliation Act of 1987. Beginning with the most recently enacted Medicare legislation, this part of the study attempts to retrace the course of development of each of the 25 Medicare hospital provisions contained in this legislation.

The second part of the study involves an analysis of Medicare legislative initiatives enacted into law in 1967, 1972 and 1984. Major Medicare legislation was enacted in each of these years under different political, economic and administrative circumstances. Together, they allow us to examine the impact of these circumstances on HCFA's legislative contributions. In this area, a strong reliance will be placed on HCFA's archival records and

Congressional documents describing the evolution of these Medicare legislative initiatives.

The third study component will buttress the information gathered from Congressional and agency historical documents, as well as analyze a second set of important related issues. It involves a series of interviews with HCFA staff, Congressional committee staff, and agency political appointees.

The final component of the study consists of two indepth case histories of major Medicare legislation. The case histories help us to examine the impact of HCFA's research and demonstration program on legislative initiation as well as how and under what circumstances a policy initiative is "reshaped" over an extended period of time to conform with political and administrative changes. Focusing on the legislative changes on two major components of the Medicare program allows us to probe more deeply into their research foundations, as well as the historical, political, economic and other factors affecting legislative changes in these two Medicare program components.

This indepth information could not be derived solely from the survey approach used in the first two study components. Information for the case histories was derived from interviews and historical documents related to the two legislative initiatives—the Medicare Prospective Payment System and the Professional Standards Review program.

Relevance to Public Administration

In the daily news media we hear a great deal about the need for "new policies—new priorities, new ideas, new departures."[14] However, what is noticeably absent is any substantive discussion on how these new policies are to be brought into being. If we take Nelson Polsby's advice and assume that "today's new legislative policies are likely to come about in ways similar to which policies were born in the past," then we can learn considerably from the study of past legislative initiatives. By identifying legislative patterns of behavior, these past legislative initiatives can serve as a "road map to the future."[15]

Such a road map might also assist those of us who want to initiate new legislative policies by preventing the misdirection of resources and pointing us toward paths that have led others to success.[16] But the primary importance for those of us in public administration with a special interest in legislative policy formulation, is that it is vital that we understand what goes on in the little black box labeled "legislative initiation." This is because in a democracy, it is essential that information be available on how government works, how decisions are made, what forces impact on policy making, and how opinions, especially those from outside the government, affect the formulation of legislative initiatives.

Limitations of This Study

It is the premise of this research effort that a number of the conventional assumptions regarding the relationship of the bureaucracy to the Congress and the President need to be reassessed and/or elaborated. As indicated earlier, because civil servants are located as they are, in intimate contact with the every day process of government, they have an excellent vantage point from which to see the need for new legislative initiatives as well as to assess the technical and administrative feasibility of initiatives. For these reasons, elected officials often need and desire the participation of the bureaucracy in the early stages of the legislative process.

The following study attempts to document and elaborate this process and employs several reinforcing methodologies to do so—quantitative analysis, interviews and a review of agency and congressional historical documents. Nevertheless, legislative causation remains a complex and ambiguous topic. It is often difficult to precisely determine which influences or past experiences have contributed to a final legislative result. This is all the more true because bureaucratic inputs are commonly obscured by the more politically visible stages in the policy formulation process.

An equally serious limitation stems from the fact that this is a case study of a single federal agency, the Health Care Financing Administration, in a single field of policy, health care. As Raymond Bauer and Kenneth Gergen observe: "the various arenas for legislative policy initiation may not be sufficiently similar to suggest concepts of a general nature." What are the conceptual similarities, for example, in the way in which foreign policy is formed, and the way in which the Health Care Financing Administration (HCFA) decides to propose a statutory change in Medicare's hospital reimbursement policy?[17]

However, the purpose of this study is not to describe the legislative role of bureaucratic agencies in all fields of policy. Rather, it is intended to demonstrate the inadequacies of theories which ignore the bureaucracy's role, as well as to provide a research framework within which other agencies can be analyzed. This framework includes:

- Identifying the stage(s) of development of legislative provisions.
- Identifying the significant actors and activities involved in the development of these provisions.
- Examining these legislative provisions to see if patterns are held constant over an historical period with different political, economic and administrative circumstances.
- Examining the agency's interactions with the Congress and the President from both a formal and an informal perspective.
- Conducting analyses on major parts of a program to determine the impact of scientific findings and how policy initiatives are "reshaped" over time to conform to political and administrative changes.

In a sense, this entire book is a framework for analysis, offering a basis for a reasonably systematic examination of both the formal and informal contributions of the bureaucracy to legislative policy initiation in a number of substantive areas. The legislative activities and patterns this research framework enables us to measure are not unique to the Health Care Financing Administration. This book should enable the reader to unravel how the legislative initiation process works in the Department of Agriculture for farm problems, in the Department of Defense for military problems, and so on. There are areas of strong commonalities across administrative agencies. Where there are differences, special measures should be developed to address those particular circumstances.

A final difficulty, and one of major proportions, is that legislative policy initiation is normally historically bound. "While the legislative process may remain constant, in any particular case, the persons and the situation yielding a decision in one given period of time are never completely replicable. The payoff of studying events under such conditions may, for some social scientists interested predominantly in the cumulative aspects of science, be somewhat limiting."[18] Under these circumstances, the best that can be achieved is to identify a pattern of behaviors in the legislative process that can serve as a 'road map' to the development of future legislative activities.

Summary

Recognizing the distinction between the role that conventional wisdom dictates that civil servants should play and the role they in fact do play in the legislative initiation process is of tremendous importance to the fields of public administration and political science. In some form, we have all contributed to this ambiguity in the role of the bureaucracy in our governmental system. We have generally wanted civil servants to be neutral yet we want them to be responsive to the political party in power. In this respect, perhaps the more important contribution of this study is to help shift the focus of attention from the normative question of "the role that civil servants ought to play" to the behavioral one of "what influence do civil servants exert on the political process?"[19]

This shift in emphasis has considerable implications for the realm of Public Administration. This study demonstrates that civil servants participate in the legislative process in ways other than to faithfully implement the laws Congress has enacted. It also shows that they "formulate recommendations for legislation, and that this is part of the function of policy-making, even that policy-making which can be done fully only at the legislative level."[20]

But the primary importance for those of us in Public Administration with a special interest in legislative policy formulation is that it is vital that we understand what goes on in the little black box labeled "legislative initiation." This is because in a democracy, it is essential that information be available on how government works, how decisions are made, what forces impact on policy making, and how opinions, especially those from outside the government, affect the formulation of legislative initiatives.

Notes

1. Arthur M. Schlesinger, Jr. and Alfred de Grazia, *Congress And The Presidency: Their Role In Modern Times* (Washington, D.C.: American Enterprise Institute for Public Policy Research, 1974) p. 2. Also, see Richard E. Newstadt, *Presidential Power* (New York: John Wiley and Son, 1960), p. 33.

2. Peter Woll, *American Bureaucracy* (New York: W. W. Norton and Co., 1963) p. 20.

3. Ibid.

4. Joel D. Aberback, Robert D. Putnam, Bert A. Rockman, *Bureaucrats and Politicians In Western Democracies* (Massachusetts: Harvard University Press, 1981) p. 108.

5. David E. Price, *Who Makes the Laws* (Massachusetts: Schenkman Publishing Co., 1972) p. 6.

6. Leonard D. White, *The Jeffersonians: A Study in Administrative History, 1801–1929* (New York: Macmillan, 1951) p. 93.

7. Steven Kelman, *Making Public Policy* (New York: Basic Books, 1987) p. 89.

8. Charles O. Jones, *An Introduction to the Study of Public Policy* (California: Wadsworth Publishing Co., 1970) p. 47.

9. Ibid. p. 47.

10. William S. Livingston, Lawrence C. Dodd, and Richard L. Schott, "A Discussion with Wilbur Cohen, former Secretary of the Department of Health, Education and Welfare," *The Presidency and the Congress: A Shifting Balance of Power?* (Austin, Texas: Lyndon B. Johnson School of Public Affairs, 1979), p. 204.

11. *Congressional Record,* United States Congress, Remarks by Senator David Durenberger, January 31, 1985, pp. S.919–922.

12. Gerald S. Gryski, *Bureaucratic Policy Making In A Technological Society* (Massachusetts: Schenkman Pub. Co., 1981) pp. 24–5.

13. Todd D. Jick, "Mixing Qualitative and Quantitative Methods: Triangulation in Action," in John Van Maanen, ed. *Qualitative Methodology* (Beverly Hills: Sage Publications, 1983) pp. 135–47. The use of multiple techniques is generally referred to as the "within method of triangulation." The "within method" of triangulation essentially involves cross checking for internal consistency or reliability. Conversely, the "between method" of triangulation tests the degree of external validity. Regardless of which method is used, triangulation is simply thought of as "the combination of techniques or methods in the study of the same phenomenon."

14. Nelson W. Polsby, *Political Innovation In America* (Connecticut: Yale University Press, 1984) p. 1.

15. Ibid.

16. Ibid.

17. Raymond A. Bauer and Kenneth J. Gergen, *The Study of Policy Formation* (New York: The Free Press, 1968) p. 206. Also see Bert A. Rockman, "Legislative-Executive Relations and Legislative Oversight,"

Handbook of Legislative Research, eds. Gerhard Loewenberg, Samuel C. Patterson, and Malcolm E. Jewell, (Massachusetts: Harvard University Press, 1985) p. 575.

18. Charles O. Jones, *An Introduction to the Study of Public Problems* (California: Wadsworth Publishing Co., 1970) p. 10.

19. Ezra N. Suleiman, *Bureaucrats and Policy Making* (New York: Holmes and Meier, 1934) pp. 3–4.

20. Paul A. Appleby, *Policy and Administration* (Alabama: University of Alabama Press, 1975) p. 7.

CHAPTER II

Out of Sight and Out of Mind: The Bureaucracy's Legislative Role in Contemporary Theory

The inventories of published research on legislative policy initiation cover a wide territory, encompassing diverse political institutions, processes, actors and actions. Because the literature has been both "prodigious and elaborate" anyone who studies legislative policy formulation can find himself lost in a myriad of theoretical frameworks.[1]

Public Administration and Political Science have traditionally concerned themselves with describing political institutions, processes and behavior. As a result, the most prominent theories today concentrate on describing the process of producing a legislative initiative by conceptualizing the linkages between the environment and the political system. These theories generally focus on political events at the social or structural level of analysis where the emphasis is placed on broad explanations of the legislative process.[2] Included here are formalistic, constitutional models, normative theories of party government, and pluralistic and elitist interpretations of American government.

Each of these theories/models has different implications as to how legislative policies are initiated and how they flow through the government system. As a whole, the problem with them is that none go far enough in explaining actual bureaucratic behavior in the legislative initiation phase. While bits and pieces of each may help to explain behavior, none of them offer an indepth explanation.

Though they are very different, these models all share an extremely broad gauged perspective on the policy making process. They are contextual theories which focus on the whole situation, background, or environment that is relevant to the legislative process. Although each perspective has merits and limitations, their level of analysis is so broad as to place them beyond the scope of this book.

More relevant is a second category which offers considerably more promise in explaining the "details" of the legislative initiation process. This literature examines legislative formulation at the political institution or individual level. Here, the emphasis is on the internal or more immediate environment inherent to the Executive and Legislative branches. Quite often, this latter category identifies the players in the legislative process concretely—for example, congressional committee chairmen, Department and agency heads, and other key legislative actors. However, for a long time, the focus of this literature was primarily on the role of the President and the Congress in the formulation of legislative initiatives. Very little attention was dirccted at the contributions of the bureaucracy to the legislative process.

Another major shortcoming of this literature is that it does not really describe what goes on inside the proverbial "black box" at the first stage of the legislative process that is labeled "initiation." As Stephen K. Bailey noted in his study of the Full Employment Act of 1946, "A major bill does not burst like a mature Athena from the head of Zeus."[3] Someone, somewhere, must call attention to a problem and successfully initiate legislation to address the problem.

In many respects, this book is a reaction to the second group of models, which have all too often overlooked or underestimated the critical, behind the scenes role of bureaucratic actors in the legislative process. A cursory glance at the policy formulation literature in any public library makes this oversight apparent. It reveals a preponderance of literature with titles such as: The President as Chief Legislator, The President and Public Policy, The Presidency and Legislation, Congress as Policy-Maker, Congress and the Presidency and similar titles.

This situation has been remedied somewhat in the last two decades by increasingly more detailed and focused studies. As a result, there has been a growing subfield of literature concerned specifically with how the bureaucracy interacts with the President and the Congress in the formulation of legislation. Political theorists such as Anthony Downs, Nelson W. Polsby, John Kingdon, Peter Woll, Gerald S. Gryski and others have made significant headway in describing the contributions of the bureaucracy to the legislative formulation process. Nevertheless, deficiencies and ambiguities remain in the literature on the precise roles and mechanisms through which the bureaucracy makes its contributions to the legislative process. More attention should be focused on the process of legislative formulation within the bureaucracy, how these processes change over time and the utility of formal and informal communications with the President and the Congress.

We currently know that those who generate legislative initiatives within the bureaucracy, the White House and the Congress do so for a variety of motives, through varying processes, and with variable effect. We also know that "in most instances, the number of people who actively participate in the process of formulating a legislative initiative is small."[4] Beyond these conclusions, it is difficult to discern clear cut patterns in the initiation stage of the legislative process.

The most promising theory to date that offers insights into the bureaucracy's role in the legislative process was advanced by Max Weber. Weber's theory on the bureaucracy, although advanced seven decades ago, continues to offer the best explanation for the role of the bureaucracy in the legislative initiation process. One of the major factors shaping contemporary politics, Weber claimed, was "the emergency of modern bureaucracy—most especially the growing state apparatus." Weber foresaw that the bureaucracy, which was "increasingly being led by technically trained, professional career administrators, would have a major impact on establishing government policies."[5]

Looking back more than a half-century later, "we can see that Weber's insights were remarkably prescient." Particularly in the advanced nations of the West, the century from 1870–1970 saw innumerable social and political changes because of an increasing growth of the bureaucracy. However, in terms of the legislative process "the most significant of these has been precisely the steadily growing power of the permanent civil servants" to influence the development and nature of legislative initiatives.[6]

"The President As Chief Legislator"[7]

Theories that purport the President to be the chief initiator of legislation can be traced to the contributions of Theodore Roosevelt and especially Woodrow Wilson which propelled the Presidency into dynamic legislative leadership. Wilson's dogma of presidential initiative in legislation was first described in his 1879 article on "Cabinet Government in the United States."[8] Wilson based his article on what was at the time a rather obscure and innocent looking provision of the Constitution that gives direction to the President to "give the Congress information on the State of the Union, and recommend for their consideration such measures as he shall judge necessary and expedient."[9]

After Wilson wrote his now historic article, one President after another failed to measure up to his hopes. Wilson's expectations were not realized until Theodore Roosevelt, concerning whom he wrote, "We must admit that he is an aggressive leader. . . . He led Congress—he was not driven by Congress." Essential to Wilson's dogma was his conviction that the President must be a party man "who has the personality and initiative" to enforce his views upon the people and upon Congress.[10]

Proponents of this perspective point out that today it is not at all an uncommon practice for a legislative initiative, complete in all its details, to be drafted within the Executive department, or even by the President or under his personal direction. The draft bill is then submitted to Congress through the chairman of the appropriate committee or some other member known to be a supporter of the Administration. This is typically followed up by Executive pressure to secure its proper consideration and its ultimate enactment into law.

Frank Goodnow, making this observation over a half century ago described it in this fashion:

> In the United States the failure openly to give to the President constitutional powers by the exercise of which he can influence the passage of legislation and the adoption of policies, has naturally led to the development of somewhat secret and indirect, if not underhanded, methods. The President cannot introduce a bill into Congress. But there is nothing to prevent him from having a bill drawn and inducing one of his supporters

> in Congress to introduce it. The President has no power to send a representative of the Administration to participate in the debates of Congress. But members of the Administration are often heard by the committees of Congress to which bills are referred, and the President may easily persuade some member of the legislature to be his spokesman on the floor of either of the houses of Congress.[11]

The emphasis in more recent literature on the President's role in initiating legislation takes this perception even further. It brings out the fact that the ultimate measure of a President's stature in the 20th century is to be found in the legislation enacted during his incumbency, rather than in his administrative actions. Today's politics are more concerned with what shall or shall not be done rather than how it shall be done. This is merely another way of saying that people are more responsive to issues of policy than to the details of administration.

Interest in the recent 1988 Presidential elections indicates the importance the American public attaches to the Presidency for the initiation of legislation. This concern was based chiefly on the policies which the various candidates were expected to follow, if elected, with respect to foreign aid, taxation, labor-management policy, farm policy, civil rights, etc. These are essentially matters of legislative policy, rather than administrative policy. These facts are familiar to everyone who reads the newspapers, though it is doubtful whether many of us realize the extent to which the habit has grown in recent years.

In his book, *The Presidency and Public Policy,* Robert Spitzer identified three general categories into which he places the literature on the President's role in taking the legislative initiative. Like the numerous studies on Presidential behavior, they mix both normative and empirical elements.

> (1) The first variant is the executive-supremacy model. It posits simply that the President is, and should be, the primary initiator and implementor of legislative proposals. Congress can modify and ratify, though it often has an obstructionist streak the President must overcome. The old axiom that "the President proposes and Congress disposes" accurately conveys what many feel is and should be the relation between the executive and the legislature.
>
> (2) Spitzer labels the second view of the relation between

the President and Congress as the Whig or strong Congress model. Simply stated, this approach contends that primary responsibility for legislative initiation does, or should, rest with Congress. The statement that the "Congress legislates, and the President executes the laws" is often used to convey this view.

(3) Spitzer's third variant of the President's role is the responsible party or party government model. The primary theme of this literature is that both the President and members of Congress should take their cues from their political parties. These cues would be based on clear cut, programmatic, specific and ideological coherent programs emanating from the parties. Presidential legislative policy leadership is still important, but it is the operation of the political party behind the two institutions that distinguishes this view from the other approaches.[12]

This discussion now leads us to question what implications this literature has for this study. In particular, what implications does it have for the role of the bureaucracy in the formulation of legislative initiatives?

It was previously indicated that, today, increasing attention is being placed on the expanded role of Presidential leadership in the initiation of legislation. In fact, the President's role as chief legislator is one of the most visible and publicized functions of his office. Richard Neustadt, for example, in an article entitled the "Presidency and Legislation,"[13] carefully documents the way in which the President has established his ascendancy over both the agenda of Congress and legislative proposals coming from his own Executive Branch.

An alternative interpretation of this situation, however, which is illustrated throughout this book, is that such perspectives tend to over personalize the Presidency. They treat the relationship of the Executive Branch to the legislature as if it were primarily or exclusively a personal relationship between the President and the Congress.

The fault with this apparent Presidential hegemony over the legislative policy formulation process is that it masks the fact that much of what ultimately comes to be regarded as the President's legislative program stems in the first instance from initiatives generated by bureaucrats. Often, these bureaucrats are at very low levels in the Executive establishment.

This lack of recognition for the contributions of the bureaucracy was validated in John Kingdon's recent study of important actors in the agenda setting process. Bureaucrats were judged to be important in only 32 percent of the interviews he conducted.[14] However, as Kingdon notes, these opinions reflect the subjective images of Washington insiders, not the actual sources for the content of the legislative initiatives. Upon further investigation, he found that career civil servants tend to have more impact on the specifications of legislative initiatives.

Others argue that the bureaucracy has an even greater impact than that indicated in Kingdon's study. Robert Spitzer, for example, in his study of Presidential initiatives, points out that a significant portion of these initiatives originate in the bureaucracy. He states that according to a recent estimate the White House Office of Management and Budget handles approximately sixteen thousand proposals annually. About 80 to 90 percent of those proposals are generated by the bureaucracy. The other 10 to 20 percent constitute legislation developed by the President and his aides in the White House.[15] Again, the key point of this investigation is to similarly quantify HCFA legislative proposals included in the President's legislative package, as well as those that are subsequently enacted into law.

Given the implications of these data, we can respond to the question raised earlier that bureaucratic "advice" can constitute a substantial part of the President's legislative initiatives. Unquestionably there is much interaction in the legislative process between the President and administrative agencies. However, it is evident that, because of the overemphasis on the role of the Presidency in this model, it offers an unbalanced perspective in describing the role of the bureaucracy in legislative policy initiation.

Does The Congress Initiate Legislation?

To confront the question directly, one might ask: Does Congress really initiate legislation? Evidence from numerous empirical investigations indicates that the Congress does indeed initiate legislation. These investigators often cite examples in Congress where committees possess life or death authority over proposed legislation. As part of the cases described in Chapter I we noted how Wilbur Mills, the former chairman of the powerful

House Ways and Means Committee, was able to successfully block Medicare legislation for almost a decade. However, once coerced on the political reality of the legislation by President Johnson, Mills and his committee gained credit as the substantive architects of the legislation. Such examples are used by Congressional proponents who "maintain that legislative policies on such matters as taxation, civil rights, welfare, and labor relations tend to be shaped in substantial part by the Congress."[16]

Despite numerous examples of Congressional legislative initiatives, the literature of discontent with legislatures in general, and Congress in particular, has reached immense proportions in recent years. While few will argue that the ability of the twentieth century American Congress to initiate legislation has declined in an absolute sense, most would agree that the position of Congress, relative to that of the President, or bureaucracy has declined.

Congressional critics maintain that this shift in the balance of power is most apparent in the declining role of Congress as an initiator of legislation and as a force for policy innovation.[17] These critics point out that the Congress now awaits legislative initiatives developed in the Executive Branch, for it is the President, they believe, who establishes much of the legislative agenda and sets priorities.[18]

Congressional proponents have not been completely passive in the face of these attacks. They point out that while the Congress has come to expect the Executive to provide them with draft bills embodying his recommendations, this does not mean that Congress always accepts the President's proposals. They argue that what the members of Congress want is "some real meat to digest."[19] Remarks by a House of Representatives committee chairman to an Administration witness in 1953 continue to be instructive on how the process works. "Don't expect us to start from scratch on what you people want. That's not the way we do things here—you draft the bills and we work them over."[20]

On the other hand, the Congressional literature contains numerous illustrations where in "certain policy areas, congressmen have done much of the legislative policy initiation."[21] A major component of the Medicare program is an example of a legislative initiative that is largely a Congressional product. In this case, Senator Wallace Bennett, at one time the Senate Finance Committee's ranking Republican, pushed a proposal for Professional Standards Review Organizations (PSROs) onto the legislative agenda and subsequently into law.[22] PSROs were composed of physician organizations in a locality which had been designated to review the quality of hospital care provided to Medicare beneficiaries. Congressional proponents point out that cases such as this occur too frequently to be considered isolated examples.

The Congress has also attempted to counter Executive and bureaucratic encroachments on the legislative initiation process by enlarging its professional staffs; establishing support agencies such as the Congressional Budget Office, and the General Accounting Office; and exploiting committee leverages to provide more effective oversight over federal administrative agencies.[23] It has also counterattacked with encroachments of its own in areas of Executive discretion. For example, a common legislative mechanism designed to use bureaucratic expertise is to require an agency to conduct scientific studies on a public problem and report to the Congress by a prescribed date on alternative means of addressing the problem.

John Kingdon's study, which was cited earlier, also provides quantitative indicators on the importance of Congress in legislative initiation. Respondents in his study judged members of Congress to be important in 91 percent of the interviews. This places them right next to the President in importance in the legislative initiation process.[24]

Senators and Representatives are discussed frequently in Kingdon's study partly because they are among the few actors in the political system who have marked impacts on both the agenda and the alternatives that are seriously considered. Of course, this does not mean that they have complete control over the agenda. Uncontrollable events, Presidential requests, and lobbying forces all impinge on the legislative agenda as well.

This makes it difficult to pinpoint any one source, including the members themselves, as exclusively in control of the legislative agendas. But members of Congress, in contrast to most other actors, have the unusual ability to combine some impact on the agenda with some control over the alternative legislative initiatives that are seriously considered.

Congressional proponents also maintain that a significant amount of "bargaining" takes place prior to a bill's submission to the Congress. "When an Administration does decide to advance a legislative initiative, staff in the Executive Branch often shape its provisions by drafting language that will smooth the way on the Hill." This is a subtle form of Congressional influence that often escapes undetected by legislative observers.[25]

Any account of Congressional policy making that involves any degree of "political bargaining" must also take account of the persistence of committees as the dominant organizational form in Congress. Congressional committees not only matter, they also differ in ways that have a considerable impact on the form and substance of legislative initiatives.

Former HEW Secretary, Wilbur Cohen, cites the Medicare program as a good example of Congressional committee sensitivity on the part of the Johnson Administration. He states that:

> . . . when I was trying to effectuate the Great Society programs, for example, working between the Executive and the Congress, I did not even think of Congress as an institution. The idea that there is sort of a unilateral or unified thing called "Congress" is a mistaken notion. The House is different from the Senate. The Senate is different from the House. The Conference Committee is different from both the House and the Senate. And if you are trying to pass legislation, you have to treat them differently. The House Ways and Means Committee is very different from the Senate Committee on Finance. You would never have treated Wilbur Mills the same way you treated Harry Byrd, the Chairman of the Finance Committee or Byrd the same as you treated Wilbur Mills. . . . you must never overlook the institutional differences among the committees in Congress.[26]

Given the importance of Congressional committees, there are aspects of Committee life that impact directly on the development of legislative initiatives in administrative agencies. If we look behind this apparent resurgence of the Congress in the initiation of legislation we also find a significant role that is played by the bureaucracy that is particularly true in the interaction of Committee staff and administrative agencies.

Most Congressional observers would agree that the influence and absolute numbers of Congressional staff have grown over the years. Many legislators, swamped with a workload of increasing bulk and complexity, have come to rely on their aides and committee staff for legislative recommendations and professional expertise.

Congressional staff have become responsible for much of the legislative work undertaken by the Congress—"organizing hearings, conducting investigations, drafting legislation, preparing Committee reports and liaison with the Executive Branch."[27] Alan P. Balutis advances these impressions further, stating that "staffers are also influential in that they have enabled the legislature to originate legislation, work out legislative ideas and amend or modify proposals emanating from the Executive Branch or interest groups."[28]

Particularly, the bureaucracy has served as a fertile source of recruitment for Congressional Committee staff. In the area of health, for example, key staff persons for Congressional committees with jurisdiction over Medicare legislative matters were recruited from HCFA (or its predecessor, the Medicare Bureau). Individuals such as Robert Hoyer, Staff Director for the Senate Finance's Subcommittee on Health, Jay Constantine, Paul Rettig and Erv Hytner, who are former Staff Directors for the House Ways and Means Subcommittee on Health, all were acquired by these Congressional committees after extensive careers with the Medicare program.

Also, outside of health care, a great many committee staff members have an extensive and often impressive background in Executive departments. In a survey conducted by Harrison W. Fox and Susan W. Hammond, it was found that 44 percent of all committee aides had worked in the Executive Branch at some point in their careers. Thirty-five percent had moved to their committee jobs directly from the Executive Branch. These recruitment patterns tended to be representative of committee staff in the Congress as a whole.[29]

Even if committee staff are recruited from other sources, they quickly find that they need to establish close working relationships with staff in various administrative agencies. This is because of the need to have a constant source of relevant, accurate and meaningful information, for which in many cases an administrative agency is the only source. In this respect, relationships of confidence with agency staffs are vital and are eagerly sought.

As a result, committee staff and agency officials who work

together on common problems eventually build up the kind of understanding which maximizes the effect of agency opinion upon committee legislative decisions. Committee recommendations in turn have a primary effect upon the content of laws passed by the parent body, the Congress. These staff-to-staff relationships are not merely a means for the exchange of information, they are also crucial opportunities for agency officials to maximize their influence on committee decisions, in this case on Medicare legislation.

In spite of its close relationship with the bureaucracy, we must also conclude that the "Congressional" model is not adequately descriptive of the role of the bureaucracy in the legislative initiation process. One of its major limitations is that it does not give sufficient recognition to the bureaucracy as a major source of ideas for inclusion in the President's and the Congress' Medicare agenda. Moreover, this literature, like the "Presidential" literature, relegates the role of the bureaucracy to the "background" of the legislative process.

The Bureaucracy's Role in Legislative Initiation

Long ago, Max Weber recognized the distinctive attributes the bureaucracy offered to modern governments. His hypothesis that "the two greatest shapers of the modern state would be the professional politician and the professional civil servant," has resulted in a growing subfield concerned specifically with their interaction.[30]

Analyzing the development of rational bureaucratic organization in the modern world, Weber points out that the "bureaucracy's superior efficiency, based on technical knowledge, makes it indispensable—giving it a monopoly of skills."[31] This means that those with formal responsibility for legislative initiatives will eventually develop an increasing reliance on the bureaucracy as a source of relevant, accurate and meaningful information.

Spurred by this theoretical activity, some scholars have given closer attention to the role of the bureaucracy in the legislative policy formulation process as well as its input into the substance of legislative initiatives. As a result, an expanding body of literature is now beginning to emerge that is focused, not just on the classic questions of bureaucratic policy formulation through administration, but also on its specific role in legislative initiation.[32]

Perhaps the most comprehensive study to date on bureaucratic influence in determining legislative policy was conducted in 1981 by Aberbach, Putnam and Rockman.[33] Their study strongly indicates that the Weberian ideal distinction between politicians who make legislative policy, and bureaucrats who merely implement it, does not realistically describe their roles in modern democracies.[34] Rather, these authors find that both engage heavily in politics, and each understands that the other plays a role in the legislative initiation process.

In their refinement of the Weberian theory, these authors introduce a very useful summary of what they refer to as the "images" of the relationship between politicians and civil servants and their respective roles in the legislative initiation process. These images and their content are recapitulated below:

> *Image I: Policy/Administrative.* This was the earliest and in many ways the simplest theory about the relationship between politicians and civil servants: "politicians make policy; civil servants administer. Politicians make decisions; bureaucrats merely implement them." Image I, which offers the starkest differentiation between the roles of bureaucrat and politician, emerged in the last half of the nineteenth century, "as the Weberian distinction between professional bureaucrats and party politicians was itself crystallizing."
>
> *Image II: Facts/Interests.* This second image assumes that both politicians and civil servants participate in making policy, but that they make distinctive contributions. "Civil servants bring facts and knowledge; politicians, interests and values." Image II, which admits a certain policy-making role for civil servants, can be, according to the writers' viewpoint, roughly dated to the beginning of the twentieth century.
>
> *Image III: Energy/Equilibrium.* According to Image III, both bureaucrats and politicians engage in policy making, and both are concerned with politics. The real distinction between them is this: "whereas politicians articulate broad, diffuse interests of unorganized individuals, bureaucrats mediate narrow, focused interests of organized clienteles." In this interpretation of the division of labor, politicians are "passionate, partisan, idealistic, even ideological; bureaucrats are, by contrast, pru-

> dent, centrist, practical, pragmatic." The writers say that Image III, which concedes to civil servants a rather more "political" role, has been extracted primarily from the writings of the last several decades.
>
> *Image IV: The Pure Hybrid.* Image IV suggests speculatively that the last quarter of this century is witnessing the virtual disappearance of the Weberian distinction between the roles of politicians and bureaucrats, producing what we might label a "pure hybrid."[35]

The authors conclude that the trend in western democracies seems to be toward a convergence of the roles of bureaucrat and politician. In this respect, they even speak about the bureaucratization of politics and the politicization of bureaucracy. However, they caution that if this sort of convergence is indeed under way, it may mark the demise of what we may call the Weberian epoch of modern government, the analytic construct from which this study began.

On the other hand, these conjectures remain speculative. Throughout the industrialized democracies today most policymakers still fall rather naturally into one or the other of our two basic categories—politicians and bureaucrats. The authors advise that while straining for a glimpse of the future, we should not mistake it for the present.[36]

In separate articles, written in celebration of the American Constitution and the administrative state, both Chester A. Newland and James P. Pfiffner gave implicit recognition to the dangers of the latter "Image" depicting the convergence of bureaucrats and politicians. They discuss the impact of the increasing reliance by Presidents on "transient political appointees for positions formerly filled by long-term professional experts." Both Newland and Pfiffner contend that the placement of political appointees at increasingly lower levels in the bureaucracy politicalizes the government and in the long term is counter productive and leads to ineffective government.[37]

Hugh Heclo and Nelson Polsby detected this trend during the Carter Administration. They noted that high ranking civil servants have been losing ground in the constellation of forces in Washington. Polsby states that "senior bureaucrats have lost ground massively."[38] This is because the functions of the federal bureaucracy have changed and because careerists are not thought to be sufficiently trustworthy by their political superiors.[39]

The Bureaucratic Power of Advice

In general, the literature in this area consistently states that to the extent that career civil servants are important in the initiation of legislative proposals, their importance can be understood as the product of several resources available to the bureaucracy. "Civil servants are alleged to have the necessary expertise, the dedication to the principles embodied in their programs, an interest in program expansion, and sheer staying power." These attributes are sometimes cited as leading them to "capture the political appointees in their agencies, to forge powerful relationships with interest groups and with members of Congress, or to shape the flow of information essential to legislative policy initiation."[40]

Whether or not these allegations about the sources of bureaucratic power are accurate, the underlying fact is that bureaucratic influence in the initiation of legislative proposals is done chiefly through the capacity of bureaucrats to give advice on legislative policy initiatives. That is, to offer support, recommendations and technical and professional assistance to the President and the Congress. We refer to Paul Light's survey on the sources of ideas for the President's legislative agenda. The bureaucracy emerged as very important. As indicated in table 2.1, 46 percent of the survey respondents identified the Executive Branch as an important source of Legislative ideas for the President's agenda.

It should also be noted that the power of bureaucrats to advise is obscured because it is indirect. This advisory power rests upon their ability to persuade political officials that a certain course of action should or should not be taken. Bureaucrats have influence only if politicians accept their advice. However, once bureaucrats have been granted the right to exercise discretion in the development of legislative initiatives, this power becomes direct.[41] The actual content of legislative initiatives may in some instances become entirely a matter of bureaucratic determination.[42]

The premise of this book is that the bureaucracy becomes intimately involved in developing suggestions on legislative policy problems which are acted upon by the White House and the Congress. This is because, generally, no part of government, and often the private sector, has more expertise about a policy area than the government organization involved in the area.

The bureaucracy employs people who work full-time in a particular policy area. For example, HCFA has devoted an entire administrative division for examining policy issues involving how eligibility for Medicare benefits should be determined. Conversely, elected officials and their staffs must divide their time over such diverse issues as health, defense and education. Agency officials are also closer to the situation. Because they are actively involved in administering a particular program, they get more ongoing feedback from the world outside government.[43]

Because of their expertise they understand the political constellation surrounding an issue better than short-term participants in the White House and the Congress. The bureaucracy is also a unique source of information on whether production capabilities exist or can be created with regard to various policy alternatives.

Table 2.1 Sources of Ideas

Source Mentioning	*Percentage of Respondents*
External sources	
Congress	52%
Events and crisis	51
Executive Branch	46
Public opinion	27
Party	11
Interest groups	7
Media	4
Internal source	
Campaign and platform	20%
President	17
Staff	16
Task forces	6

Note: Congressional staff aides were asked the following question: Generally speaking, what would you say were the most important sources of ideas for the domestic agenda? The number of respondents was 118.

Source: Paul C. Light, *The President's Agenda,* (Baltimore: The Johns Hopkins University Press, 1982) p. 86.

For these reasons, elected officials and their staffs need the participation of the bureaucracy in the early stages of the legislative process.[44]

This study demonstrates that HCFA is a major source of ideas for inclusion in the President's and the Congress' Medicare legislative agenda. The reason for this rests squarely on the resources available to the agency. As one aide in the Carter Administration described this situation:

> Despite all the complaints, the Executive Branch fills the gaps created by scarce Presidential resources. Departmental liaison is involved in the lobbying process; departmental research is involved in formulation; departmental aides are often on loan to the White House itself. The Executive Branch is involved at virtually every step of the policy cycle; the departments are asked for ideas at the start and implementation at the end. "We are dealing with a system that places a premium on bureaucratic initiatives," one Carter assistant suggested. "The Executive Branch has all the advantages. . . . the information, the manpower, the Congressional support, and the expertise."[45]

In an effort to give a more precise meaning to this description, this book explores HCFA's role in the legislative process in a more indepth fashion. This is vitally important because if we are to comprehend why legislative policies have the form they do, we must first have "some idea of the factors that converge to produce them and how they relate to each other."[46]

Notes

1. Heinz Eulau, "Legislative Research In Historical Perspective" *Handbook of Legislative Research,* Eds. Gerald Loewenberg, Samuel C. Patterson and Malcolm E. Jewell (Massachusetts: Harvard University Press, 1985) p. 1.

2. Randall B. Ripley and Grace A. Franklin, *Policy-Making In the Federal Executive Branch* (New York: The Free Press, 1975) p. 1.

3. Stephen Kemp Bailey, *Congress Makes A Law* (New York: Columbia University Press, 1950) p. 37.

4. Edward V. Schneire, *Policy Making In American Government* (New York: Basic Books, 1969) p. 5.

5. H. H. Gerth and C. Wright Mills (eds.), *From Max Weber: Essays in Sociology* (New York: Oxford University Press, 1946) pp. 232–234.

6. Joel D. Aberback, Robert D. Putnam, and Bert A. Rockman,

Bureaucrats and Politicians in Western Democracies (Massachusetts: Harvard University Press, 1981) p. 1.

7. Wilfred E. Binkley, "The President as Chief Legislator," in *Congress and the President,* ed. Ronald C. Moe (California: Goodyear Publishing Co., 1971) p. 53.

8. Woodrow Wilson, "Cabinet Government in the U.S.," *International Review,* 6 (August 1879) pp. 46–163.

9. Constitution, Article II, Sec. 3, United States of America.

10. Woodrow Wilson, *Constitutional Government in the United States* (New York: Columbia University Press, 1908) p. 65.

11. Frank J. Goodnow, *Principles of Constitutional Government* (New York: Harper Brothers, 1916) p. 121.

12. Robert J. Spitzer, *The President and Public Policy,* Alabama: University of Alabama Press, 1903) pp. 90–91.

For a more indepth discussion of party government also see David E. Price, *Bring Back The Parties* (Washington, D.C.: Congressional Quarterly Inc., 1984). This book surveys the current state of the parties and argues that "bringing the party back" is a worthy goal in light of the functions parties have played and can play in a democratic political order.

13. Richard E. Neustadt, "Presidency and Legislation: The Growth of Central Clearance," *American Political Science Review,* Vol. XLVIII (September, 1954), pp. 641–671.

14. John W. Kingdon, *Agendas, Alternatives, and Public Policies,* (Boston: Little, Brown and Co., 1984) p. 34.

15. Robert J. Spitzer, *The Presidency and Public Policy* (Alabama: University of Alabama Press, 1983) p. 5. Also see James W. Davis and Delbert Ringquist, *The President and Congress* (New York: Barron's Educational Series, Inc., 1975) p. 102. Davis and Ringquist estimate that 50–80 percent of all legislation enacted by Congress originates in the Executive Branch.

16. James E. Anderson, *Public Policy Making,* second edition (New York: Holt, Rinehart and Winston, 1979) p. 36.

17. Ronald C. Moe and Steven C. Teel, "Congress as Policy-Maker: A Necessary Reappraisal," *Congress and The President,* ed. Ronald C. Moe (California: Goodyear Publishing Company, 1971) p. 32.

18. Richard E. Newstadt, "President and Legislation: The Growth of Central Clearance," *American Political Science Review,* 48 (1954): 641–71. Also, Sam Huntington goes even further: he states that "the President now determines the legislative agenda in Congress almost as thoroughly as the British Cabinet sets the legislative agenda of Parliament." See Samuel Huntington, "Congressional Responses to the Twentieth Century," *Congress and America's Future,* ed. David B. Truman (Englewood Cliffs, N.J.: Prentice-Hall, Inc., 1965) p. 23 and Michael L. Mexey, "The Congress As An Activist Legislature," *Congress and the Presidency,* Vol. 3, No. 1, Spring 1986.

19. James Anderson, op. cit., p. 63.

20. James W. Davis and Delbert Ringquist, *The President and Congress* (New York: Barron's Educational Series, Inc., 1975) p. 103.

21. James Anderson, op. cit., pp. 64–65.

22. Subsequent law renamed these organizations "Utilization and Quality control Peer Review Organizations," commonly referred to as Peer Review Organizations (PROs).

23. Alan P. Balutis, "Legislative Staffing: A Review of Current Trends," *Legislative Staffing, A Comparative Perspective,* Eds., James J. Heaphey and Alan P. Balutis, (New York: SAGE Publications, 1975) p. 27. Balutis maintains that modern legislation is complex and technical, and comes before the legislature in a crushing quantity. Legislatures have created staff research agencies to provide them with two essential ingredients of good policy decisions: (1) accurate, thorough, relevant information, carefully analyzed from the legislative perspective, and (2) the necessary time for the legislators to apply this information and analysis accurately in evaluating available policy alternatives.

24. John W. Kingdon, op. cit., 37–8.

25. Lawrence C. Dodd and Bruce I. Oppenheimer, *Congress Reconsidered* (Washington, D.C.: Congressional Quarterly Press, 1985) p. 175.

26. William S. Livingston, Lawrence C. Dodd, and Richard L. Schott, "A Discussion with Wilbur Cohen, former Secretary of the Department of Health, Education and Welfare," *The Presidency and the Congress: A Shifting Balance of Power?* (Austin, Texas: Lyndon B. Johnson School of Public Affairs, 1979), p. 202.

27. "Expansion of Committee Staff," *How Congress Works,* Congressional Quarterly Inc. (Washington, D.C.: GPO, 1983) p. 105.

28. Alan P. Balutis, "Legislative Staffing: Does It Make A Difference," *Legislative Reform and Public Policy,* Eds. Susan Welch and John G. Peters, (New York: Praeger Publishers, 1977) pp. 132–133.

29. Harrison W. Fox, Jr. and Susan Webb Hammond, *Congressional Staffs, The Invisible Force in American Law Making* (New York: The Free Press, 1977) pp. 45, 46, and 60.

30. Michio Muramatsu and Ellis S. Krauss, "Bureaucrats and Politicians in Policymaking: The Case of Japan," *The American Political Science Review* (March 1984) p. 126.

31. H. H. Gerth and C. Wright Mills (eds.), *From Max Weber: Essays In Sociology* (New York: Oxford University Press, 1946) pp. 232–234.Also see Martin Albrow, *Bureaucracy* (New York: Praeger Publishers, 1970) p. 45. Albrow asserts that Weber was sure that rational bureaucracy was bound to increase in importance because of a series of characteristics—precision, continuity, discipline, strictness and reliability.

32. For a sample of cases on bureaucratic legislative initiation see: (1) Henry A. Foley, *Community Mental Health Legislation: The Formative Process* (Massachusetts: Lexington Books, 1975); (2) Gerald S. Gryski, *Bureaucratic Policy Making In A Technological Society* (Massachusetts: Schenkman Pub., 1981); and (3) A. Lee Fritschler, *Smoking and Politics* (New Jersey: Prentice-Hall Inc., 1981).

33. Joel D. Aberbach, Robert D. Putnam, and Bert A. Rockman,

Bureaucrats and Politicians In Western Democracies (Cambridge, Mass.: Harvard University Press, 1981).

34. An excellent discussion of the policy–administrative dichotomy can be found in Paul H. Appleby's book, *Policy and Administration,* 1975.

35. [Reprinted by permission, #90540], Joel D. Aberbach, Robert D. Putnam, and Bert A. Rockman, *Bureaucrats and Politicians In Western Democracies* (Cambridge, Mass.: Harvard University Press, 1981) pp. 4–20.

36. Ibid., p. 19.

37. See Chester A. Newland, "Public Executives: Imperium, Sacerdotium, Collegium? Bicentenial Leadership Challenges," and James P. Pfiffner, "Political Appointees and Career Executives: The Democracy–Bureaucracy, Nexus in the Third Century," *Public Administration Review,* Vol. 47, No. 1, January/February, 1987, pp. 45–64.

38. Nelson W. Polsby, "The Washington Community, 1960–1980," Thomas E. Mann and Norman J. Ornstein, eds., *The New Congress* (Washington, D.C.: American Enterprise Institute, 1981) pp. 7–31.

39. Bert A. Rockman, "Legislative–Executive Relations and Legislative Oversight," Eds. Gerhard Loewenberg, Samuel C. Patterson and Malcolm E. Jewell, *Handbook of Legislative Research* (Massachusetts: Harvard University Press, 1985) p. 524.

40. Kingdon, op. cit., p. 32.

41. An excellent example of this delegated legislative authority is contained in the recently enacted Omnibus Budget Reconciliation Act of 1987 (P.L. 110–203). A provision of this law provided that the Secretary of HHS is to conduct scientific studies on the effectiveness of flu vaccines for the Medicare population. If the Secretary determines that the vaccines are effective, Medicare coverage of these vaccines may be provided without additional legislation.

42. A distinction is made here between bureaucrats having "power" and "authority." The concept here is consistent with Max Weber's view that bureaucracy could be analyzed without prejudging the issue of democracy. That is, Weber believed that there were several devices for ensuring that bureaucratic officials are guided directly by, and answerable to, an elected assembly. For a more indepth explanation, see Martin Albrow, *Bureaucracy* (New York: Praeger Publishers, 1970) pp. 45–49.

43. Steven Kelman, *Making Public Policy: A Hopeful View of American Government* (New York: Basic Books, Inc., 1987) p. 90.

44. Ibid.

45. Paul C. Light, *The President's Agenda* (Baltimore, Md.: The Johns Hopkins University Press, 1982) p. 92.

46. Kenneth M. Dolbeare, *American Public Policy* (New York: McGraw-Hill Book Co. 1982) p. 9.

CHAPTER III

Techniques of Legislative Interaction

One of the basic aims of this chapter is to describe broad patterns of behavior in the legislative process involving the Health Care Financing Administration (HCFA), the Congress and political appointees in the Executive Branch. The central focus is on how HCFA career staff interact with political appointees in the agency, the White House, Congressional committee staff and legislators on an ongoing basis.

HCFA's relationship with these key actors in the legislative process was frequently described by interviewees—congressional, political and career—as close and mutually beneficial. But aspects of these relationships were also characterized by some as distrustful, strained and inefficient. These conflicting reports often indicate the subtlety and complexity that is often associated with the legislative process.

We present in this chapter four areas that depict that HCFA's relationship with key actors in the legislative process: (1) technical and support services provided to political appointees and the White House, (2) the independent development and advancement of legislative initiatives, (3) routine services intended to cultivate "good will" by assisting legislators to respond to requests from constituents and (4) technical and consultative services to the Congress in the development of Medicare legislative initiatives. Before we discuss the four areas of HCFA's interaction with the President and Congress, an explanation of HCFA's legislative organizational structure and how it relates to the White House is warranted.

Other researchers have reported that the White House Office of Congressional Relations often has very few political resources available to it. "The office has always been small, with fewer than ten professionals on the staff at any one time. Also, the liaison personnel rarely have substantive expertise in any issue area." This is because the "Congressional Relations Staff has usually had a rather limited role in the process of policy formulation."[1]

Given this situation, how can the White House Office of Congressional Relations overcome these disadvantages and assist the President in the passage of his legislative program? One means of doing so is to rely on departmental and agency legislative and Congressional liaison staffs. In this respect, HCFA's staff contributes enormously to the integration of the Executive and Legislative branches of government.

The focal point of HCFA's legislative activities is concentrated in its Office of Legislation and Policy (OLP). This office identifies and analyzes issues influencing HCFA's health programs and evaluates how the objectives of these programs can best be supported legislatively. The office is also HCFA's liaison with the Office of the Secretary (HHS), the White House, as well as Congressional committees concerned with health care delivery and financing programs.

Within the Office of Legislation and Policy, the Division of Legislation provides leadership and direction in the development of the agency's legislative programs. Its staff has a variety of social science academic backgrounds. The Division of Policy Analysis performs policy studies for the HCFA Administrator and integrates the results into the legislative planning process. The staff in this division generally have academic backgrounds in economics, statistics or policy analysis.

Third, OLP's Division of Legislative Services and Congressional Affairs analyzes current and pending legislation and responds to Congressional requests for information on HCFA programs. The Congressional Affairs section mainly has staff educated in the social sciences, while the legislative Services section employs primarily para-professional staff.

In total, OLP employs approximately 60 staff members. Figure 3.1 shows the formal organizational structure of the Office.

Figure 3.1 The Organizational Structure for the Office of Legislation and Policy, HCFA

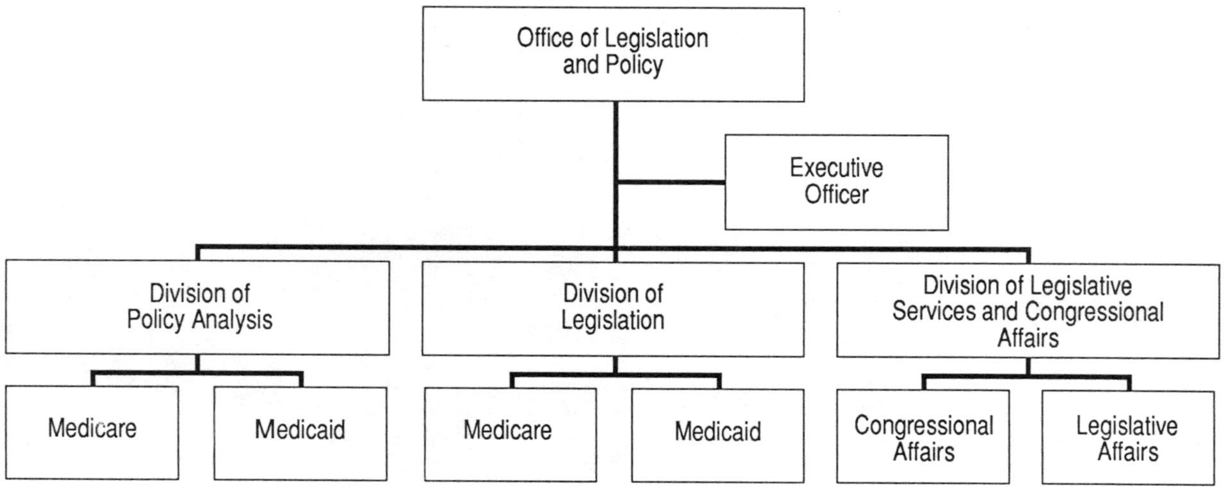

While the focus of HCFA's legislative activities is in OLP, each bureau and office also has at least one staff person who coordinates legislative activities within its component. At the beginning of each legislative cycle, these individuals solicit, screen and obtain approval of legislative initiatives in their respective bureaus or offices. These documents, typically referred to as "A-19s," represent the first formal step in the development of HCFA's legislative proposals.

Each so called A-19 contains a description of the proposal, the goal it is to achieve, a discussion of the problem with current law, a justification for the proposal, an assessment of its impact, costs, effective date and identification of key agency personnel to contact concerning the proposal. The A-19s are forwarded to OLP where they are screened, developed further, if necessary, and submitted to the HCFA Administrator for approval. The legislative package is then submitted to the Secretary of HHS and ultimately to the White House's Office of Management and Budget for inclusion in the President's formal legislative package to be submitted to the Congress.

For the most part, HCFA's legislative activities within the Executive Branch and with the Congress are integrated into its daily activities. While some periods are more intense than others, the agency's interaction with key actors in the legislative process is continuous. The following sections discuss the four areas of these relationships that were identified earlier.

The Agency's Legislative Relationship With The President

HCFA's participation in the preparation of the President's Medicare legislative package is tied to the Congressional budget process. The enactment of the Congressional Budget and Impoundment Act of 1974 established certain time frames for the Congress to comply with in formulating the federal budget. Prior to that time, only the Executive Branch prepared a formal budget for the upcoming year. The new budget procedures now serve as the means for determining not only the extent of federal financial commitment to health programs but also the substance of legislation that puts these programs in place.[2]

As part of the new budget process, the President is required to submit his budget to the Congress within 15 days after the Congress convenes—usually in late January of each year. This event culminates a budget and legislative development cycle that began nine months earlier. At the beginning of the cycle each spring, the Executive Office of Management and Budget (EOMB) solicits legislative proposals from the agency that may be advanced in the President's legislative package to the Congress. HCFA's staff develops proposed legislative initiatives in accordance with broad policy guidelines established by EOMB. This has been a routine procedure in the Executive Branch since the early 1970s.

The legislative development process in the Executive Branch for major legislative initiatives with high political appeal or controversy is typically divided into two components. One is deciding generally what should be done, if anything, concerning a particular problem. Decisions like "What reforms should be undertaken to prevent the depletion of the medicare trust funds?" would be made at the White House or have its approval before it is advanced. In other situations, there are questions such as: How strongly should the use of Health Maintenance Organizations (HMOs) be encouraged in the nation's health care system? Answers to these type of questions take the form of general principles.[3]

HCFA participates in decision making on both types of questions by assisting political officials at the White House and the Office of the Secretary in defining the problem and identifying alternative solutions. This, of course, does not preclude major legislative initiatives from being completely developed in the agency and offered as viable alternatives.

Once these broad political questions have been resolved, the second set of activities, which are generally delegated to the bureaucracy, involves more clearly defining the methods for accomplishing these goals, and often the actual drafting of the legislation. This second set of activities, involving the design of the specific legislative provisions, can have a substantial effect on its eventual administration and the actual content of legislative policy.

A good example of HCFA's contribution to the development of

major Executive legislative initiatives is President Reagan's 1982 proposal to encourage greater competition in the health care sector as a means of containing health care costs. This initiative would have provided persons eligible for Medicare benefits with an optional voucher in which to purchase private health insurance protection. In this instance, HCFA staff alerted political officials to major flaws in the initiative and suggested means for addressing these flaws. Some of the more insightful comments the agency made on the Medicare voucher proposal were:

> It is important that the Administration's pro-competition legislation be administratively feasible in addition to meeting policy objectives. These legislative specifications are fraught with administrative difficulties which can be alleviated by amending the specifications without doing harm to the basic policy objectives of the proposal. . . . We strongly believe that the HMO provision should be packaged both as part of the competition bill and the 1982 HCFA legislative initiatives. The HMO provisions should not be held hostage to what is likely to be protracted legislative debate over the competition proposal. . . .
>
> Administration of the optional Medicare voucher described in your legislative specifications is certain to be complex, difficult and costly. It substantially adds to HCFA's administrative responsibilities while taking away none. . . . If these legislative specifications are implemented, we estimate that this could require increased operational funding of over $130 million and more than 2900 additional HCFA employees to administer the program. . . .
>
> The voucher will also be very complicated and confusing for Medicare beneficiaries. The multiple premium structure and potentially large number of options will compound the beneficiary's confusion.
>
> The legislative specifications include several provisions which may produce significant adverse selection against Medicare. As a result, the voucher program may result in substantial overall cost increases rather than cost savings.

The White House subsequently abandoned the pro-competition legislative initiative. In an effort to control rising health care costs the President later proposed the Medicare Prospective Payment System. As discussed in greater depth in Chapter five,

HCFA participated extensively in the development of this legislative initiative.

"Cats and Dogs" Legislative Initiatives

The legislative initiatives developed as part of HCFA's annual legislative package cover a wide range of proposals. HCFA's legislative recommendations to the White House for FY 1988 contained forty-four A-19s for Medicare legislative initiatives. As previously mentioned, many of these legislative initiatives were subsequently included in the President's formal legislative package which is submitted to the Congress.

The primary focus of the Administration's sponsored bill, H.R. 2864, was to make cost reductions and administrative improvements in the Medicare program. Twenty-three of the bill's 45 provisions could be traced to HCFA's legislative recommendations. The number HCFA initiated is thought to be higher since the bill also contained agency proposals that were submitted in prior years that were not available to this research.

There are some agency proposals, that are generally not considered significant enough for inclusion in the President's formal legislative package. These proposals are submitted to the Congress separately in what is often referred to as the "cats and dogs" bill.

Annette Coates, an agency employee responsible for coordinating the "cats and dogs" bill describes these proposals as low impact legislative initiatives that are usually designed to address some administrative problem(s) or to improve administrative efficiency. "These are not earth shaking proposals," she states "but are significantly more than minor or technical corrections to the law." "Cats and dogs" come from agency staff who have contact with Medicare fiscal intermediaries, hospitals and beneficiaries in the course of their jobs. These employees frequently discover administrative problems that require changes in the Medicare law.

"Cats and dogs" are typically non-controversial proposals with negligible or no cost. As a practical matter, time pressed political appointees generally give these proposals lower priority since they are usually very technical, involving the "nuts and bolts" of the problem they are designed to address. However, each proposal does require the "concurrence" of all affected agency components before it is advanced as a legislative initiative.

Using these criteria, we can see that the last 3 provisions enacted as part of the 1987 Medicare amendments (table 3.1) would be included in the "cats and dogs" category. That is, they were not included in the President's formal legislative package, had low or negligible cost, and were judged to have low political controversy.[4]

Two provisions (Sections 4001 and 4031) with low or moderate political controversy that were not included in the President's

Table 3.1

Title: Executive Generated Provisions in the 1987 Medicare Amendments by Cost, Inclusion in the President's Formal Legislative Package and Degree of Political Controversy.*

*Executive Generated Sections***	*Costs (in billions)*	*Included in President's Package*	*Political Controversy**
(4002)	$ – .180	Yes	High
(4006)	– .180	Yes	High
(4066)	.000***	Yes	High
(4049)	.000	Yes	High
(4031)	– .530	No	Moderate
(4001)	– .410	No	Low
(4009a)	.000	No	Low
(4012)	.001	No	Low
(4014)	.000	No	Low

*Political controversy was judged by the degree of controversy expressed during committee hearings, whether it was highlighted in a Presidential message, minority report, floor debate, etc.

**Descriptions of these sections include: 4002—Hospital Prospective Payment Rate Increase, 4006—Reduction in Payment for Hospital Capital, 4066—Payment to Hospital Outpatient Departments for Radiology, 4049—Fee Schedules for Radiologist Services, 4031—Payment Cycle Standard, 4001—Extension of Reduction under Sequester Order, 4009a—Responsibilities of Medicare hospitals in Emergency Cases, 4012—Payments for Hospital Services, and 4014—Civil Money Penalties Against HMOs.

***This provision would produce no cost/savings in FY 1987, but would have significant savings in subsequent years. ($30 million in 1988, $40 in 1989 and $5 in 1990.)

legislative package were excluded from the cats and dogs category because they provided for significant Medicare program savings. The first of these provisions (Sec. 4001) extended for three months the sequester order imposed by the President reducing Medicare payments to hospitals by 2.3 percent.

The second provision (Sec. 4031) imposed minimum time frames before Medicare payments could be made to a hospital. The effect of this provision was to slow the disbursement of funds from the Medicare Trust Funds which would allow additional interest to be accrued. These provisions are not considered as "cats and dogs," but as significant agency legislative proposals.

When we view the spectrum of agency activities in the development of the President's legislative program, the evidence overwhelmingly indicates that the agency is deeply entrenched in the legislative development process in the Executive Branch. It participates in major legislative decisions by helping to define problems and by identifying alternative solutions. As demonstrated in the development of President Reagan's Medicare Voucher proposal, HCFA is also a key resource for alerting political officials of major flaws in Presidential legislative initiatives and in suggesting means for addressing these flaws. Finally, the agency is responsible for developing a substantial part of the President's Medicare legislative package as well as a variety of low impact legislative proposals.

Dealing With Congress: An Integrating Influence

An important by-product of HCFA's relationship with the President and the Congress is that it contributes enormously to the integration of the Executive and Legislative Branches of government. HCFA staff interacts with political appointees in the agency, the Department of Health and Human Services, the White House, Congressional committee staff and legislators on an ongoing basis. These relationships provide much of the cement that binds the Legislative and Executive Branches together. Evidence presented in this study shows that HCFA is a primary source of information for legislative staff members. Reciprocally, agency staff frequently used their Congressional contacts to keep abreast of Congressional activities involving the Medicare program.

These lateral relationships provide a means of achieving coordination or accommodation outside of what Emmette Redford has termed the "traditional model of democratic administration." As Redford notes, "in the American polity, administration is not a function solely of the Executive Branch; it is a continuing function of both the Legislative and Executive Branches, exercised through parallel hierarchies in the two Branches interacting with each other." Within the web of political-administrative activity described by Redford, "decisions often are made in a consensus process which merges the Executive and Legislative Branches in a manner in which neither is in charge."[5]

The aspects of executive-legislative integration examined in this study include HCFA's efforts to cultivate goodwill among legislators and provide technical and consultative services on legislative issues.

Cultivating Goodwill

It is apparent to most political observers that it would not be prudent for HCFA to wait until a specific legislative proposal is advanced before it begins to cultivate harmonious relations with legislators. To this end, HCFA employs a continuous process of legislative liaison with the Congress. The extent to which such good will contributes positively to Congressional receptivity of agency legislation is difficult to measure quantitatively. Nevertheless, the agency considers this an important function and has given it a high profile and considerable access to agency resources.

A good part of Congressional liaison activities, according to Carleen Talley, Director of the Division of Legislative Services and Congressional Affairs, is precautionary. That is, it is intended to keep legislators from becoming "annoyed" with the agency. It is also part of HCFA's attempt to "cast bread upon the waters" and to maintain a reservoir of good will.

This cultivation of good will can be found at all levels of the agency; however, it is most prominently seen among the agency's higher echelons who make visits to Congressional offices to address their concerns. HCFA's ten regional offices usually work with congressmen at the local level. At HCFA's central office in Baltimore/Washington where the Congressional liaison machinery is more elaborate, the focus is on agency-wide problems and key members of Congress. These Congressional contacts range from briefings on implementation activities for major pieces of legislation to alerting a congressman of a research or demonstration project that will take place in his district.

The increasing importance in "cultivating good will" by federal agencies in general was originally documented by J. Leiper Freeman in 1955. Its importance is reflected in the sizeable staffs and high ranking officials who spend a substantial portion of their time on this function.[6] HCFA's Congressional Affairs staff has 12 employees devoted to this function on a full time basis. However, as previously indicated, all HCFA bureaus and offices are equipped to consider requests from Congressional offices and to furnish them information speedily.

The thrust of the Congressional Affairs Staff's operations is to provide a single source of information to members of Congress on agency activities. When a staff person receives a request from the Congress, he or she gathers the necessary information to respond, rather than refer the Congressional staffer to several different offices to obtain the needed information. In total, the Division of Legislative Services and Congressional Affairs handles over 1100 telephone inquiries a month, conducts numerous Congressional office visits, directs congressional correspondence to the appropriate agency component and provides briefing sessions on agency functions and activities for members of Congress and their staffs.

Relationships with Congressional Staffs

Because much of the meaningful work of legislative bodies is done in committees rather than in full legislative assemblies, HCFA's relationship with the Congressional committees having jurisdiction over its programs is crucial to the success of its legislative initiatives. Congressional committees having legislative jurisdiction over the Medicare program include the Subcommittee on Health, Senate Committee on Finance; the Subcommittee on Health, House Committee on Ways and Means; and the Subcommittee on Health and the Environment, House Committee on Interstate and Foreign Commerce.

These committees decide the fate of almost every Medicare bill that is introduced in the Congress. In acting on any particular Medicare legislative initiative, the committees may approve the bill, thus practically assuring its passage by its respective chamber. The committee may also alter the bill, fail to report on it, reject it outright or even write a new bill. While each house has the machinery for "calling out of committee" bills that have been "pigeonholed" or "buried," as well as for rejecting the recommendations of a committee, in most instances the committee's decision stands.[7]

Frequently, the most easily accessible and knowledgeable people with the committees are the professional staffs. As indicated earlier in Chapter two, Congressional staff often serve as the fiduciaries for members of Congress. It is also generally agreed that the more knowledgeable the Congressional staff member is on Medicare issues, the more influential he/she is with the committee.[8] This is because knowledge and information constitute an independent source of power on the "Hill."

This knowledge enables experienced Congressional staff to influence the drift as well as the technical details of Medicare legislation. The staff's job, as described by Wilbur Mills, the former Chairman of the House Ways and Means Committee, is to "bring facts together for our use, to do the spade work for us." "This also involves digging into the minds and moods of the Congressmen who will actually do the voting."[9]

Informal working relationships are eagerly sought after by both agency and committee staffs. Both political and career agency staff consistently reported in the interviews that contacts between committee and agency staffs are often frequent and mutually beneficial.

Practically all of the interviewees reported that most of the contacts are of a technical nature and are handled with a great deal of mutual sensitivity for each other's perspective. The benefit to the Congressional staffer in these relationships is an easily accessible source of information and data in a timely fashion. To the uninitiated Congressional staffer, HCFA's bureaucracy is not only massive, but resembles a maze when one is seeking a specific source of information. Thus, it is extremely useful to have a knowledgeable and trusted person inside the agency to obtain the needed information rather than to sort through the organizational maze to find the appropriate person.

For the agency, the benefit of these informal working relationships with Congressional staff is being kept abreast of Congressional activities involving the Medicare program and being involved in the legislative process. The frequency of contacts can range from several times a day when legislation is being formulated, to once a week or less when legislative activities are at a lull.

Technical Assistance to the Congress

One of the most misunderstood notions about bureaucratic participation in the legislative formulation process involves the activities associated with providing "technical assistance" to the Congress. To the lay person, "technical assistance" often conveys an image of assisting someone with minor details or on the technical means of accomplishing some task. However, this term has a broader context when it is applied to the legislative formulation process. In the legislative context, it often includes the actual drafting of legislation, providing advice on alternative means of achieving goals and determining whether proposals are administratively feasible.

Appendix #1 demonstrates a typical example of the technical assistance the agency provides to the Congress. This proposal was initially drafted in the Congress and referred to HCFA for "technical" comments to ascertain whether the proposal actually does what the committee intended to do. HCFA was also asked to determine if there were more efficient administrative means to accomplish the proposal's objectives. Appendix #2 shows that the provision, as enacted into law, includes essentially all of the agency's "technical" comments.

What these exhibits demonstrate is that HCFA also has a significant role in the fashioning of legislative proposals developed outside its organizational boundaries. The extent of these services, of course, varies with each legislative initiative, but judging from similar examples and personal interviews, it is extensively employed throughout the legislative process.

In summary, HCFA's relationships with the Executive and Legislative Branches contribute enormously to the integration of these two branches of government. Agency staff interacts with political appointees, the Department of Health and Human Services, and the White House on an ongoing basis. The principal contacts agency staff have with the Congress is through the "cultivation of good will" or through contacts with respect to gathering information about legislative proposals. Through these contacts, committee staff and agency officials, working together on common problems, build up the kind of understanding that maximizes the effect of agency opinions upon committee decisions. Committee recommendations, in turn, are the primary determinants upon the content of laws passed by the Congress.

There is general recognition among political analysts that bureaucratic participation in the legislative process is indirect. That is, it rests upon the agency's ability to persuade elected officials that a certain course of action should or should not be taken. In this sense, HCFA has influence only if politicians and their aides choose to accept their advice.

Building upon this knowledge, this study reveals that HCFA staff performs a full range of legislative services for the President and the Congress. These services include investigating and defining problems, researching and commenting on legislation, providing advice on alternative means of achieving goals and determining whether proposals are administratively feasible.

The evidence is clear that HCFA's "advice" is often a significant factor in fashioning legislative proposals initiated by the President and the Congress. In many cases, the actual content of legislative initiatives is entirely a matter of bureaucratic determination. It is also clear that HCFA is often an independent initiator of legislative proposals.

Notes

1. Eric L. Davis, "Congressional Liaison: The People and the Institutions," *Both Ends of the Avenue,* Edited by Anthony King, (Washington, D.C.: American Enterprise Institute for Public Policy Research, 1983) p. 76.

2. Stephen E. Lawton, "Special Report, Budget Reconciliation," *The New England Journal of Medicine,* November 19, 1981, Vol. 305, No. 21, pp. 1297–1300.

3. James E. Anderson, *Public Policy-Making,* Second Edition, (New York: Holt, Rinehart and Winston, 1979) p. 66.

4. These three provisions provided for: more strenuous enforcement and penalties in cases where hospitals/physicians violate Medicare requirements in the treatment of emergency cases (Sec. 4009a); repeals the option for HMOs to have Medicare reimburse hospitals directly (Sec. 4012); and, provides civil money penalties to HMOs who fail to provide medically necessary care (Sec. 4014).

5. Emmette S. Redford, *Democracy in the Administrative State* (New York: Oxford University Press, 1969) pp. 70–81. Also see Alan P. Balutis'

interpretation of Redford's statements in "The Role of the Staff in the Legislature: The Case of New York," *Public Administration Review,* (July/August 1975), p. 359.

6. J. Leiper Freeman, *The Political Process, Executive Bureau—Legislative Committee Relations* (New York: Doubleday, 1955) p. 162.

7. Samuel Steinberg, *Understanding American Government and Politics* (New York: Keystone Education Press, 1972) p. 35.

8. See Charles C. Francis and Jeffrey B. Trammell, *The Almanac of the Unelected: Staff of the U.S. Congress, 1988* (Lanham, Md.: University Press of America, 1988). This comprehensive reference book profiles the top 600 Congressional staffers in the U.S. House of Representatives and the U.S. Senate. The profiles include the staffer's professional background and expertise, legislation in which the staffer has played a significant role, ideological or political orientation, unique contributions the staffer has made to the legislative body and opinions of colleagues and observers on the staffer.

9. Arlen J. Large, "Help on the Hill," *Readings in American Government,* Editors: H. Malcolm MacDonald, Wilfred D. Webb, Edward G. Lewis and William L. Strauss (New York: Thomas Y. Crowell Co., 1968) p. 309.

CHAPTER IV

Changing Patterns of Legislative Interaction

This chapter takes a long-term perspective of HCFA's interactions with the President and the Congress. To get a barometer of how HCFA adjusts its legislative program to environmental changes, we examined several key indicators: (1) trends in the agency's consultation with the Congress, (2) the origin of Medicare legislative initiatives and (3) the primary impact of those initiatives.

The evidence presented shows that HCFA has the ability to shift its legislative activities and behavior in accord with changes in budgetary needs, political sentiments and social demands. These changes are reflected in the type of interactions the agency has with political appointees and the Congress, as well as in the focus of its Medicare legislative initiatives. The data in this chapter also bring into question the widely held assumption by many political observers that the agency, and the bureaucracy in general, are primarily interested in program expansion.

We have also explored those resources and information available to HCFA that virtually assure its participation in the legislative process. Evidence from the study shows that these resources and the agency's problem solving capability give it significant influence in the legislative process.

Trends in Congressional Consultation

One of the most formidable obstacles confronting research of this sort is getting an accurate measure of the level of consultation on legislative matters that takes place between HCFA and the Congress. Consultation is an elusive term that can take many

Table 4.1

Title: The Amount of Documented Congressional Consultation With HCFA Staff on Legislative Provisions for 1987, 1984, 1972 and 1967.*

Year	*Total Number of Legislative Provisions*	*Number of Legislative Provisions With Documented Consultation*	*Percentage of Legislative Provisions With Documented Consultation*
1987	25	2	8%
1984	27	13	48%
1972	19	13	69%
1967	22	18	81%

*Consultation in this context means that evidence of formal or informal written communication was found. It is recognized that oral (as well as documents not available to the researcher) communication constitutes a significant part of HCFA and Congressional consultation.

* * * * * *

forms, although in the context of this study it refers to documented evidence of either formal or informal communication.

It is recognized that oral communication (and documents not available to this research) can also constitute a significant part of HCFA and Congressional consultation. Despite these definitional and documentation problems, the instruments used in this study provide an informative barometer for determining the level and types of legislative consultation that take place between HCFA and the Congress.

The primary sources for this information on legislative "consultation" are agency briefing books compiled by the Office of Legislation. Legislative briefing books are used to familiarize agency officials testifying before Congress on legislative issues affecting the Medicare program. Historically, these books have contained documentation on all relevant agency and Congressional activities related to a hearing and descriptions of the various Medicare legislative provisions under active consideration by the committee.

An examination of Table 4.1 on the amount of documented

Congressional consultation with HCFA shows that there has been a constant decline in this material since 1967. In 1967 evidence of Congressional consultation was found on 81% of the Medicare amendments. This percentage decreased to 69% in 1972 and to 48% in 1984. Documented evidence of Congressional consultation was only found on 8% of the legislative provisions in the 1987 Medicare amendments. Despite the increasing decline of formal documentation in the later years of the study, particularly for 1987, all of the interviewees acknowledged that extensive legislative consultation continues to take place between HCFA and the Congress. This leads us to conclude that the data collected in this study are suggestive but hardly conclusive, that the communications between agency and committee staff have declined.

Supporting evidence from the interviews indicates that the instrument used to measure consultation (i.e., primarily legislative briefing books) became less effective over time. Explanations offered by interviewees suggest that several reinforcing trends contributed to the changes in Congressional consultation. These trends include: changes in the type of information contained in the legislative briefing books, increased levels of distrust between the Congress and the President and the growth of Congressional staff and support agencies.

One of the explanations for this paucity of easily accessible documentation was given by Carleen Talley, Director, Division of Legislative Services and Congressional Affairs. She attributed it to the desire for more concise briefing material from Dr. William Roper, the HCFA Administrator at that time. Talley stated that Dr. Roper required that discussions on individual provisions in legislative briefing books be condensed to the minimum number of pages. Typically 1 or 2 pages are used for each legislative provision. Therefore, a briefing book on the 1987 Medicare amendments, with 25 provisions affecting hospitals, would only consist of approximately 50 pages. Agency legislative briefing books for previous Administrators on comparable legislation would have required a two inch binder.

Talley's explanation helps to explain the dramatic decline in documented evidence of Congressional consultation in 1987. However, the downward trend for 1972 and 1984 are not explained by this factor. Interviews with other agency and Congressional staffs revealed continued Congressional consultation with HCFA on various legislative provisions. At a minimum, this involved requests for technical legislative support or requests to obtain HCFA's position on legislative proposals, however, these contacts were decreasingly reflected in the agency's legislative briefing books.

Some interviewees speculate that this paucity of documented evidence on Congressional consultation can also be attributed to an increasing level of distrust by the Congress in the information and motivations of political appointees in the agency. One interviewee commented that the committee has been known to send a legislative package to HCFA with strict instructions that political appointees are not to review the package. This was because the request was for "technical" assistance and not a request for a policy position. The intent of the committee in this instance was to obtain agency "technical assistance," while limiting access to the legislation by political appointees whom it was feared might use the information for political purposes.

It would appear reasonable to conclude that the increasing level of distrust can be attributed, in part, to divided party government. The reader will note that the last three study years—1987, 1984 and 1972—are years with Republican Presidents and Democratic control of at least one house of Congress.

One Congressional staff member expressed the level of distrust in this fashion:

> There is less trust of political appointees than of career people. By and large, civil servants have a greater tendency to carry out congressional intent of legislation. Political appointees try to manipulate the law to meet their policy objectives.
>
> HCFA's data are always verified. The consensus on the committee is that they have been tempered to fit the Administration's political policy. This was less true in past years.

Agency career staff express similar concerns:

> Yes, there is a lack of trust in Congress of political appointees. When the "Hill" really wants to get down to business they know how to circumvent political appointees.
>
> I believe that the agency people are more trusted on the "Hill." They simply explain legislative proposals and their consequences. Political appointees must defend them.

Conversely, a former HCFA political appointee provides another view:

> The lack of trust depends on your perspective. If the data aren't what the Congress wants to see, the out-cry is that its been doctored. For example, when the Congress was considering expanding Medicare to cover people with end-stage renal disease, the actuaries said that it would be very expensive. Congress claimed that the figures were doctored for political ends. In retrospect, we can see that the actuaries were right.

Another political appointee pointed to the survival of the Professional Standards Review Organizations (PSRO) Program as a justification for their suspicions of the motivations of some career officials. He said that the evaluations of the PSRO Program were not definitive of its effectiveness. This led President Reagan in 1981 to conclude that overall control of health services utilization and cost had been ineffective through the regulatory approach provided by PSRO review.

At the urging of then OMB Director, David Stockman, President Reagan proposed to remove the federal requirements for PSRO review, and to support only the most effective PSROs for a two year transition period. It was theorized that the effective PSROs would become a component of the competitive market by contracting their services to private health care systems.[1]

The interviewee, as well as several others, attributed the survival of PSROs during the early Reagan years to the efforts of a key career agency official who capitalized on the lack of uniform criteria for judging the success of the PSRO Program. Despite drastic budget cuts and a lack of definitive data to support retaining the review organization, this careerist launched a "private" campaign to save the fledgling PSRO Program. It was reported that over the objections of his superior political appointees, he surreptitiously lobbied key members and staff in the Congress, convincing them of the usefulness of PSROs. As a result of these efforts, the almost certain death of the PSRO Program was temporarily stayed by the Congress.

Recognizing this and similar situations, James L. Scott, former HCFA Deputy Administrator, was later to comment that "some careerists want to be free to carry out their own political agenda, regardless of which political administration is in the White House. We simply could not tolerate this situation."

Another interviewee characterized the PSRO situation in this fashion:

> . . . the agency people were considered the real experts by the Congress—and they had their own biases. It's often an interpretation of whether the glass is half empty or half full. It's really the interplay between the agency and Congressional staff that defines the "reality" of a proposal. Perhaps the lesson to be learned here is that the President may propose legislation, but it is the agency people who must explain it and respond to questions from the "Hill". For this reason, the proposal actually becomes what ever agency officials define it to be.

Another possible explanation for the decline in documentable evidence of Congressional consultation with HCFA is the growth in Congressional professional staff and support agencies. The increase in professional staff has been well documented; most notably by Susan W. Hammon.[2] Also the number of Congressional support agencies involved in analyzing HCFA programs has increased considerably. These support agencies include organizations such as the Congressional Budget Office (CBO), the Prospective Payment Assessment Commission (ProPAC) and the Office of Technology Assessment (OTA).

Following the logic of this explanation, these additional resources available to the Congress would make it less dependent upon HCFA for technical consultation. One interviewee reported that it also makes the Congress highly suspect of HCFA's motivations when it is provided with inconsistent or conflicting information from that provided by Congressional staff agencies.

Critics of this growth in Congressional agencies contend that they essentially duplicate policy components in HCFA, and that their sole purpose is to "provide a secondary covering for the Congress." One observer capsulized this argument by stating "it gives them the ability to say that someone else, the experts, have recommended a particular course of action. It's a simple way of justifying what they want to do by padding their positions."

It is clear that the reasons for the decline in documented evidence of consultation between the Executive and Congressional Branches of government are multifaceted. Nevertheless, from a public perspective, perhaps it is more important to ascertain the impact this condition has upon how the American government operates, regardless of its cause. In the legislative area, many of the interviewees believe that the effects are already obvious—resulting in a more cumbersome and complex legislative process with considerable distrust of each other's motives.

Shifts in The Origin of Medicare Legislative Initiatives

It is reasonable to assume that if there have been changes in the type of interactions HCFA has had with the President and the Congress, that these changes would also be reflected in the origins of enacted Medicare legislative initiatives. To determine if this is the case, we first examined the origins of the hospital provisions included in the Medicare amendments for 1987. We then determined if these findings remained constant over the 20 year period covered by the study.

Agency legislative briefing book data and A-19s which identify the sources of the 1987 Medicare hospital legislative provisions indicate that 36% of these provisions had their origin in the Executive Branch (see Table 4.2). Forty-four percent are attributed to the Congress and 8% to other sources.[3] A closer examination of the nine provisions enacted in 1987, which are exhibited in Table 4.3, reveals that the origins of 88.8 percent of the Executive generated legislation could be traced to HCFA.

Table 4.2

Title: Origins of Medicare Hospital Provisions in the Omnibus Budget Reconciliation Act of 1987

Genesis	*Number*	*Percentage*
1. Executive Branch	9	36%
2. Congress	11	44%
3. Other	2	8%
4. Missing data	3	12%
Total	25	100%

*****

Table 4.3

Title: Relationship Between Medicare Hospital 1987 Amendments, the President's 1987 Legislative Package, and HCFA Initiated Proposals.

	President's Legislative Package			
*Section ***	*Included in Bill*	*Not in Bill*	*HCFA Initiated*	
4001	no	yes	no	
4002	yes	no	yes	
4006	yes	no	yes	
4009(a)	no	yes	yes	
4012	no	yes	yes	
4014	no	yes	yes	
4031	no	yes	yes	
4049	yes	no	*	
4066	yes	no	*	
	4	5	8	
	(44.4%)	(55.5%)	—	(100%)

*HCFA developed the original proposal at the direction of the White House/HHS. It was significantly modified by the Congress.

**Descriptions of these sections include: 4002—Hospital Prospective Payment Rate Increase, 4006—Reduction in Payment for Hospital Capital, 4066—Payment to Hospital Outpatient Departments for Radiology, 4049—Fee Schedules for Radiologist Services, 4031—Payment Cycle Standard, 4001—Extension of Reduction under Sequester Order, 4009a—Responsibilities of Medicare hospitals in Emergency Cases, 4012—Payments for Medicare hospitals in Emergency Cases, 4012—Payments for Hospital Services, and 4014—Civil Money Penalties Against HMOs.

Moreover, 55 percent of the Executive generated provisions were not included in the President's formal legislative package submitted to the Congress.

The proportions of legislative provisions for the Legislative and Executive Branches sections in the 1987 Medicare hospital amendments have not been constant historically. An examination of the primary sources of Medicare legislation spanning a 20 year period reveals a decreasing proportion of enacted Medicare legislative initiatives originating in the Executive Branch. This downward trend in Executive generated Medicare legislation is accompanied by an increasing proportion of legislation having its genesis in the Congress.

Table 4.4 shows that over 72 percent of the amendments in the 1967 Medicare legislation had their origins in the Executive branch. Several senior interviewees attributed this high percentage to the need to fill "gaps" in Medicare coverage, extend Medicare entitlement to previously "overlooked" aged population groups and to make administrative "refinements" in the relatively new Medicare program. The political influence of then Social Security Commissioner Robert M. Ball also contributed significantly to this high percentage. (Commissioner Ball's influence will be discussed in greater detail shortly.)

In 1972 the percentage for Executive generated legislation fell to 47.3%. In 1984 it was 29.6%. There was a slight increase in 1987 with 36 percent. Conversely, the Congressional generated provisions constituted only 4.5% in 1967, 36% in 1972, and increased to 44% in 1984 and 1987.

Several interviewees attributed the higher percentage of Congressional generated legislation in 1984 and 1987 to the high rejection rate of politically unpalatable proposals offered by the

Table 4.4

Title: Origin of Medicare Hospital Legislative Provisions
for 1967, 1972, 1984 and 1987.

	YEAR			
Genesis	*1967*	*1972*	*1984*	*1987*
Executive	16 (72.7%)	9 (47.3%)	8 (29.6%)	9 (36%)
Congress	1 (4.5%)	7 (36.8%)	12 (44.4%)	11 (44%)
Other	1 (4.5%)	1 (5.2%)	2 (7.4%)	2 (8%)
Missing	4 (18.1%)	2 (10.5%)	5 (18.5%)	3 (12%)
Total	22	19	27	25

Table 4.5

Title: Percent of Enacted Executive Generated Medicare Hospital Proposals Included in the President's Formal Legislative Package by Year.

	PRESIDENT'S LEGISLATIVE PACKAGE	
Year	*Included*	*Not Included*
1967	31.2%	68.8%
1972	88.8%	11.2%
1984	50%	50%
1987	44%	55.6%

******

Reagan Administration. These initiatives often included proposals designed to increase Medicare beneficiary cost sharing and to reduce payments to health care providers. While the final legislative package for these years provided for significant program savings, the concerns of the Congress appeared to have been how these savings were achieved and who was impacted. Percentages on legislative proposals generated from other sources remained relatively constant.

In Table 4.5 we examine these data in greater depth. This table reveals two significant highlights that are apparent in the 1967 and 1972 data. In the 1967 Medicare amendments nearly 70% of the Executive generated legislation was not included in the President's formal legislative package. Conversely, in 1972 nearly 90% of these provisions was included in the President's Formal legislative package.

One possible explanation for this significant reversal is provided by two long term HCFA careerists, Alvin Freedman, former Director, Office of Legislation, and Charles Booth, Director, Office of Reimbursement Policy. Both Freedman and Booth attribute the high proportion of the Medicare 1967 provisions not included in the President's legislative 1967 package to the strong influence of then Social Security Administration Commissioner, Robert M. Ball. Ball was described as a politically independent administrator who by-passed ineffective White House legislative clearances.

Freedman describes Commissioner Ball's administration in this fashion:

> "Bob Ball's personal influence with key members of Congress and staff gave us a great source of indirect power on the "Hill." There were very few agency, Departmental or White House clearances needed for legislative proposals that had Ball's approval. The Bureau of the Budget wasn't a big clearance factor in those days."
>
> "Our staff routinely wrote floor speeches for congressmen defending Medicare proposals. House and Senate committee staffers called individual agency legislative staff directly for consultation. There was no clear Executive-Congressional legislative separation. These things were not done surreptitiously, but were encouraged by both the Executive and the Congress as an efficient way of getting things done."
>
> "Ball had a very young, committed and idealistic legislative staff who sometimes worked seven days a week for months. Staff viewed their work as a "mission." This was a philosophical effort, our motives were not for career ambitions but for achieving the goals of the Medicare program."
>
> "When Nixon was elected and Bob Ball left in the early 1970's, his successor did not inherit his power base. Nixon brought in political and other career people who began to seize control over the legislative clearances process."

Several of the more senior interviewees corroborated Freedman's statement. The general assessment was that through reorganization, realignment of staff functions and other devices, the Secretary of Health and Human Services and Bureau of the Budget (later renamed Executive Office of Management and Budget) were no longer simply "holding companies" for the agency's Medicare legislative initiatives. By increasing the need to work with the Secretary and EOMB in order to "clear" legislation before it goes to the Congress, HCFA has become more of an extension of the White House legislative development process—losing much of its original "free wheeling independence."

Richard P. Nathan corroborates this explanation in his book, *The Administrative Presidency.* Focusing on the president as a manager during the Nixon Administration, he states that "one high level account in 1972 noted that President Nixon, distrustful of bureaucracy . . . built a kind of defense against it—and in doing so built his own bureaucracy." He states that as the White House staff grew, "new staff members became involved at increasingly lower levels in the agencies." According to Nathan, this increase in White House staff led to an increase in the "oversight role of domestic programs, routine legislative matters, as well as for many purely administrative decisions." White House clearance was "required on more and more issues and became harder to obtain."[4]

These circumstances demonstrate how HCFA is able to recognize its changing functional reality within the Executive branch. This is particularly evident in how the agency adjusted its legislative activities to respond to three different political administrations and to vastly different budgetary and political climates. As we observed, during the Johnson Administration in 1967, the origin of over 68% of the Medicare enacted amendments were not included in the President's formal legislative package. Information derived from interviews and agency briefing books indicate that these agency generated proposals were transmitted directly to the Congress.

As previously noted, this was at a time when there were few budgetary restraints and virtually no White House clearances. It was also a period in which both the Congress and the White House were under Democratic party control. Agency career staff reported an exceptionally close and open relationship with the Congress in the development of legislative initiatives.

HCFA's sensitivity and ability to work within political constraints are particularly evident during the Nixon (1972) and Reagan (1984 and 1987) Administrations. For example, in 1972 under a President who was highly distrustful of the motivations of the bureaucracy, nearly 90% of the Executive Branch's provisions were originated from the agency. The majority of these provisions originated in the agency. We also noted that over 88 percent of the Executive proposals enacted in 1987 were initiated or had substantial modifications made in HCFA.

These findings give added credence to the findings discussed in Chapter III which demonstrate how HCFA was able to work with the Reagan administration on the development of its pro-competition proposal. These examples show how the agency is able to work with the politically responsible Chief Executive, even when that Executive is distrustful of its motivations.

Table 4.6

Title: The Relationship Between the Genesis of Medicare Legislation and their Primary Impact for 1987, 1984, 1972 and 1967

	Enhance Benefits	*Program Savings*	*Improve Admin.*	*Medical Delivery*	*Study*	*Payment Equity*	*Number/ Total %*
Executive							
1987	0	55.5%	11.1%	33.3%	0	0	9/100%
1984	0	37.5%	37.5%	12.5%	0	12.5%	8/100%
1972	0	55.5%	11.1%	22.2%	11.1%	0	9/100%
1967	68.7%	0	6.2%	25%	0	0	16/100%
Congress							
1987	0	8.3%	8.3%	8.3%	16.6%	50%	1/100%
1984	0	0	63.6%	18.1%	0	18.1%	11/100%
1972	57.1%	14.2%	14.2%	14.2%	0	0	7/100%
1967	100%	0	0	0	0	0	1/100%
Other							
1987	0	0	0	0	0	100%	2/100%
1984	0	50%	0	50%	0	0	2/100%
1972	100%	0	0	0	0	0	1/100%
1967	100%	0	0	0	0	0	1/100%

Shifts in The Impact of Medicare Amendments

Perhaps the most important indicator of HCFA's adjustment to political, budgetary and social circumstances is the type of legislative initiatives it advances. Examination of this indicator is particularly important given the commonly held assumption that HCFA, and the bureaucracy in general, is primarily interested in program expansion and job preservation. In a fashion similar to the previous section, we will begin by examining the 1987 Medicare amendments and then look at this indicator over a longer period.

When we examine the relationship between the genesis of the 1987 legislative provisions and their primary impact we discover an interesting balancing feature. As demonstrated in Table 4.6, we observe that the major portion of the Executive Branch legislative initiatives (55.5%) were directed at producing program savings. This Executive cost containment emphasis is counterbalanced by

Congressional initiatives where 50% of the provisions are focused on improving the equity in Medicare program payments among health care providers.

The Executive Branch emphasis on program savings is explained by the overall thrust of the Reagan 1987 Medicare legislative package to improve the financial stability of the Medicare trust funds. This emphasis, which was also the focus of the Congressional budget process, was considered necessary to assure the continued financial stability of the Medicare program. Again, we see that while the final legislative package provided for significant program savings, the concerns of the Congress appeared to be how these savings were achieved and who was impacted. It is apparent from the data that the Congress was sufficiently concerned to assure the equitable distribution of Medicare payments among providers for an otherwise reduced reimbursement pool.

Neither the data nor the interviews yield any obvious explanation as to why such initiatives did not emerge from the Executive Branch. The reader should also note that there were no legislative provisions enacted to enhance Medicare benefits or expand program entitlements to additional population groups in 1987.

Few definitive patterns are revealed by examining the relationship between the genesis of Medicare legislative provisions and their primary impact over the four years under study. One indication, however, that deserves additional investigation is that with the exception of 1967, the greatest proportion of Executive generated provisions were concerned with producing program savings. In 1987 these proposals represented 44% of the Executive legislation that was enacted, 37.5% in 1984 and 55.5% in 1972. There were no Executive proposals enacted in 1967 to produce program savings.

As previously mentioned, the 1967 amendments were enacted during a period when there were relatively few budgetary restraints. These amendments were primarily directed at improving Medicare coverage, extending benefits to previously "overlooked" aged population groups and to make administrative "refinements" in the relatively new Medicare program.

The second largest legislative percentage for the Executive Branch fluctuates between proposals to improve program efficiency and those directed at changing the way health care services are delivered. That is, to institute mechanisms to improve the delivery of health care services, combat fraud and abuse, etc. . . . Part of the explanation for this fluctuation is that during two of the years in the study, 1984 and 1987, the Medicare program was in a major financial crisis.

Another possible explanation for this emphasis is that three of the study years—1972, 1984 and 1987—were under Republican Administrations. According to some interviewees, these Administrations were primarily concerned with restraining the growth of the Medicare program and reforming the inflationary patterns in the health care delivery system.

These findings bring into question the commonly held assumption that the bureaucracy is primarily interested in program expansion. Considerable political and budgetary sensitivity is demonstrated by the bureaucracy in the advancement of legislative initiatives. For example, in 1967, a period of few budgetary restraints, over 68% of its legislative initiatives were for program enhancements. In later years, under more austere budgetary circumstances, the agency focused on initiatives for program savings and administrative efficiency.

We observed in the previous chapter that the techniques of agency interaction with the White House and the Congress are well established. However, HCFA's legislative relationship with the Congress has not been static. Available evidence suggests that it is a dynamic relationship that has evolved markedly over the past 20 years due to changes in program life cycles, personal attributes of various Administrators, political tensions resulting from divided party government, and the development of independent staff and analytical resources in the Congress.

The extent to which technical and consultative services provided to the President and the Congress varies according to the type of legislative proposal, and the balance between formal and informal consultation. While the activities of both the Congress and the Office of the President have changed markedly over time, HCFA's multifaceted contributions to the legislative process continues to be extensive.

Notes

1. Carolyn K. Davis, Administrator, Health Care Financing Administration, Statement before the Subcommittee on Health, Senate Finance Committee, U.S. Congress, March 23, 1984.

2. See Susan Webb Hammon, "Legislative Staffs," *Hand Book of Legislative Research,* Editors: Gerhard Loewenberg, Samuel C. Patterson and Malcolm E. Jewell, (Cambridge, Mass.: Harvard University Press, 1985) pp. 273–320.

3. Note: The source(s) of the remaining 12% could not be identified.

4. Richard P. Nathan, *The Administrative Presidency* (New York: John Wiley and Sons, 1983) pp. 34–37.

CHAPTER V

The Impact of Research And Policy Analysis

One of the major objectives of this study was to determine the extent to which HCFA's research and demonstration efforts are used in developing new legislative proposals. The definition of "scientific" research was divided into two aspects for purposes of this analysis. Our first definition refers to formal social science research. This implies the use of hypotheses and the development of theories as well as the gathering of evidence to test these generalizations.

Second, we define policy analysis as employing a variety of normative and descriptive techniques to illuminate policy choices. Policy analysis assists legislators by showing more clearly what different choices entail, and what outcomes will result from what actions.

The evidence from this chapter suggests that the use of formal social science research and legislative development is not an orderly process. Instead, the findings from formal research serve more to direct our mode of thinking about public issues. That is, the findings from HCFA's formal research program appear to be targeted toward basic reforms of the health care system rather than being inextricably linked to the legislative process.

Conversely, policy analysis permeates the activities of the agency and the legislative process. These findings raise fundamental questions about our expectations for the use of formal research in the legislative process. It also suggests that the penetration of policy analysis into the legislative process has caused profound changes in how decisions are made.

The Usefulness of Formal Research In Legislative Development

Over the past two decades an increasing number of social scientists and legislators have become concerned about the usefulness of government supported social science research to the legislative formulation process. There is mutual interest in whether federally sponsored social science research intended by Congress to influence policy is actually "used" in that fashion.[1] At its root, the assumption held by these theorists and policy makers is that to be useful, good research should marry political awareness, cost-consciousness and administrative ability with scientific and statistical expertise. However, a compatible marriage of these features is often difficult to achieve in a research project.

When asked to assess the impact of formal social science research on legislative formulation, most interviewees indicated that the relationship was not direct. That is, research findings do not necessarily follow an orderly process which translates them directly into legislative initiatives. As demonstrated in Table 5.1, there is only a small or no direct relationship between the genesis of a legislative proposal and the use of formal social science research.

In explaining the lack of a direct relationship between research and the development of legislative initiatives, Dr. George Schieber, Director, Office of Research, believes that the relationship is low for several reasons. Chief among them is that the "course of action indicated by the research may not be a viable political choice." In this respect, political, financing and timing considerations frequently preclude action predicated on research findings. Research projects are also begun for "symbolic reasons, or to delay making a decision."[2] It is apparent that in such cases there would be little or no relationship to legislative initiation.

Dr. Schieber also points out a frequently overlooked benefit of research. He maintains that "research is just as effective if it disproves a course of legislative action under Congressional consideration." For example, it was the results of research findings that dissuaded the Congress from enacting a prospective payment system for hospital-based physicians in 1987 (i.e., radiologists, anesthesiologists and pathologists). He said that "while the Medicare Prospective Payment System (PPS) for hospitals was very successful, a similar system for physicians would have been a disaster. It would have been confusing to Medicare beneficiaries, caused considerable resentment from physicians and caused an administrative nightmare."

Former Deputy HCFA Administrator, James L. Scott, concurs with Schieber's assessment of the lack of an orderly process leading from research to legislation. However, he points out that for "legislation with broad social and program impact, the relationship between research and legislative development is more direct." The largest expansions or program reforms involving Medicare have had a foundation in formal research. The Medicare Prospective Payment System for hospitals, coverage of hospice services, and Medicare payment on the basis of Diagnostic Related Groups for nursing home services were all legislative ini-

Table 5.1

Title: The Relationship Between the Genesis of Legislative Provisions and the Use of Social Science Research or Policy Analysis—1987, 1984, 1972 and 1967.

	Formal Research	*Policy Analysis*	*Research General Knowledge*	*Provides Study*	*None*	*Number/ Percentage*
Executive						
1987	0	77.7%	0	0	22.2%	9/100%
1984	0	25%	25%	0	50%	8/100%
1972	0	80%	0	10%	10%	10/100%
1967	5.5%	83.3%	0	11.1%	0	18/100%
Congress						
1987	0	42.8%	28.5%	0	28.5%	7/100%
1984	0	25%	41.6%	0	33.3%	12/100%
1972	0	85.7%	14.2%	0	0	7/100%
1967	0	100%	0	0	0	1/100%
Other						
1987	0	50%	0	0	50%	2/100%
1984	0	100%	0	0	0	2/100%
1972	100%	0	0	0	0	1/100%
1967	0	100%	0	0	0	1/100%

tiatives based upon formal research funded under HCFA contracts.

Looking at national health policy over the past fifteen years, Lynn Etheredge found evidence to support Scott's perspective. Etheredge traced the significant influence of health services research in expanding government and private sector efforts to come to grips with health care financing and delivery and cost containment issues. She found that a number of major federal initiatives during this period—in health professions training, prepaid capitated delivery systems such as health maintenance organizations, utilization review, health planning—stemmed from health services research.[3]

Nevertheless, the Congress has continued to express concerns about the legislative usefulness of HCFA's research activities. Congress recently directed the General Accounting Office (GAO) to examine the relevance of HCFA's research and evaluation studies to Congressional needs. In brief, the GAO found that:

> Mandated reports from the Office of Research and Demonstrations (ORD) were often not fully responsive to Congressional needs, were frequently late and were variable in their technical adequacy. . . . Several factors affected the quality of research and evaluation studies. Within the Office, relevance was hampered by lack of communication to better understand Congressional intent in some generally worded [Congressional] mandates. Timeliness was improved by shortcuts in procurement, but technical adequacy was weakened by planning that did not include Congressional interest. . . . Outside the Office, relevance was affected, in some instances, by after-the-fact report reviews for policy compliance. Timeliness notably decreased because of a report review and revision process that involved HCFA, HHS, and the EOMB. Technical adequacy in some cases was affected by policy [political] influences during the external review and revision process.[4]

In response, agency officials argue that HCFA has developed and implemented a very effective demonstration and experimentation program. They contended that the agency's research program has had a significant impact on both the Medicare and Medicaid programs. Interviews from this study suggest that this impact is reflected in administrative and policy changes, as well as legislative and regulatory changes. Agency officials believe that the GAO concentration on whether HCFA is following correct procedures on identifying direct links to the legislative development process overlooks the basic question of whether the substance of the research and evaluation program has merit.[5]

Many of HCFA's research efforts are targeted to achieving a foundation from which basic reform of the health care system can be carried forward. Such long-range efforts require time to bring innovative project designs from the developmental stage to full implementation (hospital rate-setting and hospital uniform reporting systems being cases in point).

Testifying before the Oversight Committee, House Committee on Ways and Means, agency spokesman, Dr. James Kaple, questioned whether it is appropriate to expect that demonstration and experimentation activities (or social science research in general) should provide direct and unambiguous answers to legislative and policy issues. He stated that the broader and more far reaching importance of experimentation is in its impact on overall thinking about policies and issues in the health care sector.[6]

Research projects seldom have conclusions available that bear directly and explicitly on the legislative issue at hand. Therefore, the important question in judging the value of research is not whether it has always provided direct and unambiguous answers to policy or legislative questions, but whether it informs the Congressional debate with new knowledge and/or changes the nature of that debate.[7]

These two arguments clearly show the paradox involved in the use of scientific research and legislative policy making. In the words of David Calligridge and Colin Reeve, in their book, *Science Speaks to Power:*

> . . . as the complexity of the problems has increased, decision makers have come to be ever more dependent on the results of scientific investigations and yet it has become increasingly clear over recent years that attempting to use science in this way can generate severe problems for all concerned—policy makers and scientists alike. Science is, in reality, far from the happy servant of policy so often depicted.[8]

Perhaps the most frequent way formal social science research enters the policy arena is through what Carol Weiss refers to as "enlightenment." From her perspective it is not the findings of a single nor even of a body of related studies that directly affect policy. Rather, it is the concepts and theoretical perspectives that social science research has engendered that permeate the policy making process.[9] Simply stated, "when the findings and the intellectual structure of evaluation begin to shape the way that decision makers think about an issue—and the elements of it that they think about—evaluation has been used."[10]

One of the most frequently cited examples of the usefulness of research to the legislative process is the Medicare Prospective Payment System (PPS). This new hospital payment system vividly illustrates how the availability of a knowledge base accumulated over many years, as a direct result of impressive health services research efforts, assisted in the development of legislation that changed the direction of the nation's health care system. A brief review of this new program shows how HCFA's research efforts contributed to the development of this legislation.

The Medicare Hospital Prospective Payment System

A cursory review of the legislative history providing for the Medicare Prospective Payment System (PPS) would lead one to assume that it has a relatively short history that began with Congressional efforts to solve the Medicare financing crisis. On the contrary, the Medicare PPS program was the culmination of over a decade of HCFA sponsored research and demonstrations to develop a more effective administrative mechanism for controlling health care costs.

When the Medicare program was enacted in 1965 the payment method for hospitals adopted by the Congress was modeled after the prevailing private health insurance practices at that time. These practices generally involved retrospective cost-based reimbursement. That is, hospitals were reimbursed for any reasonable costs incurred in providing covered medical care to Medicare patients.[11]

It was not long, however, before those who were administering the program became keenly aware that this cost based reimbursement system, among other factors, contributed to the extraordinary inflation in Medicare spending. Between 1967 and 1971, Medicare hospital expenditures rose from $2.66 billion to $5.16

billion—an average annual rate of 18 percent, compared to a 5 percent annual rise for the same period in the Consumer Price Index, which measures the economy's overall rate of inflation.

Although these increases were due, in large part, to the increased access to health care provided by the Medicare program, the increases in Medicare hospital expenditures prompted HCFA researchers to focus on the development of alternative hospital payment mechanisms. This search was for a payment mechanism that would be more effective in controlling costs while continuing to make health care available to an increasing beneficiary population.[12]

In the meantime, to temporarily suppress the overall rate of inflation, the Economic Stabilization Program was enacted in 1971. This program also temporarily slowed the rate of increase of hospital costs. When the temporary program was terminated, hospital inpatient costs began rising rapidly once again. Between 1974 and 1977, federal health care expenditures rose by more than 50 percent to a level four times as high as it was in 1967.

HCFA's research and experimentation on cost-containment strategies were intensified. In 1975 HCFA funded eight state demonstration projects that instituted mandatory and voluntary health cost control programs. The most promising of these demonstrations later proved to be the project in the State of New Jersey to develop a hospital prospective rate setting program based on a hospital's patient case mix.

The New Jersey project was based on earlier research conducted at Yale University under a grant from the National Center for Health Services Research. Up to this point, the Yale research was intended not to become the basis for any sort of reimbursement scheme, but simply to help hospitals improve internal management.[13]

Responding to continued high rates of inflation, in 1978 President Carter proposed mandatory hospital cost control measures. This proposal was the brain child of then Secretary Joseph Califano who instituted a vigorous public campaign to convince the public and health care community on the need for its enactment. The proposal would have instituted cost controls on the amount of hospital cost increases that would be recognized by Medicare and Medicaid, as well as private insurers. Califano was widely quoted as describing the hospital community as "bloated and inefficient."

Paul Rettig, a former Congressional committee staff member, recalls that the Carter proposal is an example of a well conceived legislative proposal with major opposition from the hospital industry and lukewarm Congressional support. Rettig says that the "hospital industry was united in their efforts to defeat the proposal; we could tell it was dead upon arrival."

Commenting on the Carter health care cost containment proposal, John Kingdon in his book, *Agendas, Alternatives, and Public Policies,* quoted a key Congressional staffer as stating:

> This particular piece of legislation is not near and dear to the heart of anyone on Capital Hill. The ones that favor it, favor it only out of a sense of obligation and duty, out of a sense that they must do something about cost inflation, and out of loyalty to the White House. This sense of obligation and loyalty could carry the president's initiative as far as agenda status, but could not restrict the range of alternatives to his proposal that were seriously considered.[14]

What arose from the ashes of the Carter proposal was a system of voluntary cost-control efforts by the hospital sector that reduced the rate of increase in hospital expenditures. However, these controls proved to be only temporarily effective. One year later, Medicare hospital expenditures were rising even faster than they had been before—and, as the proportion of elderly in the population continued to increase, the insolvency of the Medicare Hospital Insurance Trust Fund was forecast for the end of the decade.

In response to these continuing concerns, the Tax Equity and Fiscal Responsibility Act of 1982 (TEFRA, P.L. 97-248) set limits on Medicare reimbursement for hospital operating costs on a per-case level, adjusted for each individual hospital's case-mix. Rettig commented that "this legislation was basically the brain child of the academic community, HCFA and key committee staff members." This legislation was essentially based on what HCFA had learned from interim findings from its cost containment research activities. He said that "compared to the Carter proposal, it attracted very little attention and, in retrospect, was a much more significant shift from the traditional Medicare payment methodology than what would have been established under the Carter proposal."[15]

In addition, TEFRA required that HCFA develop, in consultation with the Senate Committee on Finance and the House Committee on Ways and Means, a legislative proposal for Medicare payment to hospitals, skilled nursing facilities, and—to the extent feasible—other providers, on a prospective basis.

In February 1982, then HCFA Administrator, Carolyn Davis, responding to this legislative mandate, appointed a Task Force to develop specific methodologies that could be used in developing a prospective payment system. The Task Force was composed of HCFA staff and consultants from outside government. After several months the Task Force produced a report that applied the vast amount of knowledge obtained through HCFA's cost containment research projects. To this end, the formal report submitted to the Congress states:

> This report on Prospective Payment for Hospitals Under Medicare [was] developed in consultation with the Senate Committee on Finance and the Committee on Ways and Means of the House of Representatives. . . .
>
> This report is the direct result of several months work and analysis but draws heavily from nearly a decade of research and demonstrations by the Health Care Financing Administration, as well as other components of the Department of Health and Human Services. The Department has also benefitted by discussions with health care industry representatives as well as Congressional staff involved in health care.
>
> Thus, it is with considerable deliberation and with a rich history of research and demonstrations that the Department submits a Hospital Prospective Payment Plan. . . .[16]

In presenting the Hospital Prospective Payment Plan to the Congress, Reagan Administration witnesses marketed the plan's scientific basis, its equity for all hospitals, efficiency of operations, simplicity in payment and continued access to quality medical care by Medicare beneficiaries. The proposed plan was enacted virtually intact by the Congress on April 20, 1983 as part of the Social Security Amendments of 1983—within three months after it was submitted to the Congress.

The new Medicare hospital payment system contained four essential characteristics:

- First, payment rates are related to diagnostic-related groups (DRG's) which classify patients into groups that are clinically coherent and homogeneous with respect to resource use.[17]
- Second, the payment rates for any individual hospital are not automatically determined by the level or pattern of its present or past incurred costs or charges;
- Third, these payment rates constitute payment in full for all covered services provided a Medicare patient; and
- Fourth, each hospital keeps the difference between the payment rate and its cost for that unit of care.[18]

In summary, despite success stories like the Medicare Prospective Payment System, concerns continue to exist among policy makers about the need to have a more orderly relationship leading from research to legislative development. These concerns will not be put to rest easily. In fact, these proponents often argue that the Medicare Prospective Payment System is a good example of what can be achieved if social scientists and political actors collaborate more closely.

The fault with this analogy is that it fails to give sufficient recognition to the fact that research findings must also contend with powerful economic, political and social factors. Perhaps the main point to be raised here is to recognize that in judging the value of research, our perspective must be broadened to include its impact on the overall thinking about public policies rather than limited to its direct impact on the development of legislation.

Policy Analysis, A Viable Alternative To Formal Research?

While there appears to be no orderly process leading from formal research to legislation, it does seem clear that policy analysis permeates the activities of the legislative process. As demonstrated in Table 5.1, policy analysis typically has the highest percentage of the five categories involving research in the legislative process. Moreover, the greatest percentage of this analysis was linked to Executive Branch policy initiatives. Very few legislative initiatives were directly linked to formal research or demonstrations.

In a separate research project, Edward C. Banfield found similar evidence of the growth of policy analysis in the Executive

Branch. He also found that this growth has been paralleled by a comparable growth in policy analysis in the Legislative Branch. This is exhibited through the growth of professional staff and recently established Congressional agencies such as the Congressional Research Service, the Office of Technology Assessment and the Congressional Budget Office.[19]

Interviews with career, political and congressional staffs also validate that decision makers have a voracious appetite for information gathering and analysis. One interviewee inferred that HCFA's greatest contribution to the legislative process is "information." To this end, HCFA has dedicated an entire bureau, the Bureau of Data Management, solely to the function of gathering data, analyzing facts and figures and processing information. Since knowledge is often a source of power and influence in the legislative process, this is a tremendous resource for HCFA.

In this respect, policy analysis serves as a useful tool in the legislative process since its purpose is to:

- define and clarify objectives,
- describe alternative means to ends,
- assess benefits and costs,
- take account of uncertainties,
- quantify what looks useful to quantify,
- isolate decisions that can be deferred from those that can't, and
- create options for policy makers.

Here the focus is on limiting analytical efforts to what is possible, given political, economic and social circumstances affecting what is feasible for people and institutions to achieve. Policy choices are illuminated by showing legislators more clearly what those choices entail, and what outcomes will result from what actions.

This type of policy analysis is referred to by Alice Rivlin as the "common sense approach to decision making." The result in the legislative process is that it has replaced the "back-of-the envelope guess work on the impact of a particular proposal and has allowed legislators to focus on the real issues."[20]

Reflecting on the findings in the preceding section, on how research has been used in the legislative process, leads us to conclude that there is a need to modify our expectations about research utilization. Clearly, in the American political system the results of research are only one among many factors that decision makers must legitimately consider in the formulation of legislative policy.

As J. Fred Springer describes it, policy makers have "obligations to honor past commitments, to balance opposing values, and to respond to the political give and take that is part of the institutional cement of our pluralistic system." If research findings do not translate directly into action in this setting, it does not necessarily mean that the research has failed.[21] It does, however, lead us to question whether the use of formal research in the legislative process necessarily leads to optimal health policy.

Herein lies the benefit of policy analysis to the legislative process. While it is rarely recognized as contributing "new ideas" to the policy debate, it is an extremely useful tool in transforming existing ideas into acceptable initiatives in the legislative process. Using the medical peer review concept we can see how policy analysis was used in reshaping this well established concept into a legislative initiative that evolved into the Professional Standards Review Organization (PSRO) Program.

The case presented below illustrates how the use of policy analysis in both the Executive and Legislative Branches of government is well suited as a problem solving device that can be used in conjunction with the political process.

The Evolution of Peer Review in the Medical Community

Early Regulation

The modern concept of reviewing health care practices to determine the quality of care has evolved over a period of approximately 60 years. It was not until the late 1950s, however, that it became important for physician peer review groups to examine the appropriateness of care, as measured by the need of patients to be admitted to the hospital or to continue to stay there after they had received "necessary" care.

The stimulus for this development came, in part, from a concern over the rise in health care costs and an awareness that a great deal of health insurance money spent for hospitalization could have been saved if some patients had been hospitalized for shorter periods or treated as out-patients. To a lesser degree, it also stemmed from a consensus on the part of hospitals and the medical profession that there be a systematic effort to continually address quality assurance issues in the hospital setting.[22]

In 1959, Blue Cross of Western Pennsylvania, the Allegheny County Medical Society Foundation, and the Hospital Council of Western Pennsylvania initiated the first sustained program of "utilization review," a term they coined. This and subsequent programs were designed principally as retrospective analyses of individual hospital records. Problems identified by medical staff utilization review committees were to be corrected by educating physicians about their unnecessary utilization of services. The committee would also recommend to the hospital management changes that would eliminate inefficiencies which prolonged a patient's hospital stay.[23]

The Beginning of Federal Involvement

The first significant federal role in quality assurance began in 1965 with the establishment of the Medicare program. This legislation adopted this concept and made the operation of a utilization review (UR) program a condition for hospital participation in the Medicare program. In implementing this provision, the then Medicare Bureau issued UR regulations with the requirement that after an initial hospital stay of 12 days, and at periodic points thereafter, a patient's attending physician had to certify that continued hospitalization was "necessary" and "appropriate." If the committee found that the hospital stay was unnecessary, it could recommend to the insurer that the hospital not be paid for these unnecessary services. Each hospital's UR program varied greatly in structure, operation and effectiveness.[24]

From the inception of the Medicare program, the agency received a constant stream of criticism that UR committees represented a "fox in the chicken coop" arrangement. That is, hospitals were asked to police their own utilization behavior. In the early 1970s with Medicare costs almost double initial expectations and utilization review programs perceived to be ineffective, the Medicare Bureau began to investigate the feasibility of an outside mechanism to examine the appropriateness and necessity of hospital services for Medicare beneficiaries.

Some UR critics argued for the development of federal evaluation and audit teams to check the necessity of hospital services rendered. In contrast, the American Medical Association (AMA) argued that these evaluations required local physician judgment and proposed that State medical societies develop area-wide review programs.

Another option was offered by several local medical organizations in California, called "foundations for medical care." These foundations, which provided prepaid health services, were often in direct competition with the Kaiser Health Plan and used outside medical review mechanisms to control their expenditures. In contrast to the "after the fact" approach to medical review, these programs emphasized "concurrent" review. The intent was the prevention of further program expenditures for unnecessary hospitalization.[25]

Senator Wallace Bennett, the then ranking Republican on the Senate Finance Committee, melded the AMA proposal with the local review program concept of the foundations into a set of proposed amendments to the Medicare statute. The Bennett proposal formed the basis of the Professional Standards Review Organization (PSRO) legislation enacted in 1972.[26]

The PSRO legislation that was enacted in 1972 created a nationwide network of physician-run organizations which had final authority to grant or deny payment for care rendered to patients under both Medicare and Medicaid. Although their organizational details were complex, their essence was simple: "PSROs were to review each hospital case with particular emphasis on whether the admission was appropriate and whether the length of hospitalization was necessary."[27] The actual review process was much like the utilization review system from which it evolved.

In summary, this study supports previous research showing that policy analysis has become a useful tool in legislative formulation. It also shows that HCFA is a primary source for much of the data gathering, analysis and figures used by both the Executive Branch and the Congress on Medicare issues. This, in itself, virtually assures HCFA a role in the formulation of legislative initiatives, since it has been previously demonstrated in this research and others that knowledge and information constitute an independent source of power in government.

On this basis we may conclude that the agency has been a significant actor in investigating Medicare problems and revealing their complexities. It does not suggest, however, that the choices available to legislators have become any easier. But many legislators feel that the clarification of choices alone is a tremendous help. In this respect, the penetration of policy analysis in the legislative process has resulted in profound changes in the ethos of how decisions are made.

Notes

1. Carol H. Weiss, "The Many Meanings of Research Utilization" in Eleanor Chelimsky, *Program Evaluation: Patterns and Directions* (Washington, D.C.: The American Society for Public Administration, 1985) pp. 203–211.
2. Carolyn Ban and Elysa Ferrara, "Expanding the Concept of Utilization: Case Studies in the Organizational Uses of Evaluation," Unpublished paper, 1988.
3. Lynn Etheredge, "Government and Health Care Costs: The Influence of Research Policy," *From Research Into Policy* Editor: Marion Ein Lewin, (Washington, D.C.: American Enterprise Institute for Public Policy Research, 1986) pp. 7–20.
4. General Accounting Office, *HCFA Research: Agency Practices and Other Factors Threaten Quality of Mandated Studies,* A Report to the Chairman, Subcommittee on Human Resources and Intergovernmental Relations, Committee on Government Operations, House of Representatives, GAO/PEMD-88-9, (GAO: Washington, D.C., June, 1988).
5. HCFA comments on the GAO Report "Management of and Results Obtained from HCFA Demonstration and Experiments," HRO-80-96, Dated July 14, 1980.
6. James Kaple, Ph.D., Director, Office of Research and Demonstrations, Health Care Financing Administration. Testimony given on May 8, 1980 before the Subcommittee on Oversight, House Committee on Ways and Means, on the Management and Results of HCFA's Demonstrations and Experimentation Programs.
7. Ibid.
8. David Collingridge and Colin Reeve, *Science Speaks To Power, The Role of Experts in Policy Making,* (New York: St. Martin's Press, 1986) p.ix.
9. Weiss, "The Many Meanings of Research Utilization," op. cit., p. 209.
10. Carol H. Weiss, "Evaluation for Decisions: Is Anybody There? Does Anybody Care?," *Evaluation Practice,* Vol. 9, No. 1, February, p. 17.
11. *Report to Congress: Impact of the Medicare Hospital Prospective Payment System,* 1984 Annual Report, Department of Health and Human Services, Health Care Financing Administration, Office of Research and Demonstrations, Pub. No. 03231.

12. Ibid.

13. Joel Menges, "From Health Services Research to Federal Law: The Case of DRGs," *From Research Into Policy,* Editor: Marion Ein Lewin, (Washington, D.C.: American Enterprise Institute for Public Policy Research, 1986) pp. 20–33.

14. John W. Kingdon, *Agendas, Alternatives, and Public Policies,* op. cit., p. 26.

15. Also see Richard Sorian, *The Bitter Pill, Tough Choices in America's Health Policy,* (New York: McGraw-Hill, 1988) pp. 105–123.

16. Richard S. Schweiker, Secretary, Department of Health and Human Services, *Report to Congress, Hospital Prospective Payment For Medicare,* December, 1982, p. vii.

17. Richard F. Averill, DRGs, Diagnosis Related Groups, Fifth Revision, Document No. 9015-06-01, (Connecticut: Health Systems International, 1988) pp. 1–7.

18. Richard Schweiker, *Report to Congress, Hospital Prospective Payment For Medicare,* Department of Health and Human Services, December, 1982.

19. Edward C. Banfield, "Policy Science as Metaphysical Madness," *Bureaucrats, Policy Analysts, Statesmen: Who Leads?* Editor: Robert A. Goldwin (Washington, D.C.: American Enterprise Institute for Public Policy Research, 1980) pp. 1–20.

20. Alice Rivlin, *Systematic Thinking for Social Action* (Washington, D.C.: The Brookings Institution, 1971) pp. 12–70. Also see E. S. Quade, *Analysis For Public Decisions* (New York: Elsevier, 1976), pp. 10–12.

21. J. Fred Springer, "Policy Analysis and Organizational Decisions" *Administration and Science,* (February, 1985), p. 490.

22. "Introduction," *Medical Care,* 17: 1–5, August, 1979.

23. Ibid.

24. "Introduction," *Medical Care,* op. cit., (also see the Social Security Amendments of 1965).

25. "Introduction," *Medical Care,* op. cit.

26. See the Social Security Amendments of 1972, Report of the Committee on Finance to Accompany H.R. 1, September 26, 1972, pp. 254–268.

27. Helen Smits, "The PSRO In Perspective," *The New England Journal of Medicine,* 305:253–259, July 30, 1981.

CHAPTER VI

Conclusions: Toward A Better Understanding of Our Polity

It is obvious to most political observers that the formulation of legislative policy is a collective endeavor. It involves a host of participants—both governmental and non-governmental. Because of this, an exact determination of the contributions of the Congress, the President, the bureaucracy and interest groups in general, or on a particular piece of legislation, is virtually impossible.

Notwithstanding the obvious obstacles that confront any attempt to assign "credit" for legislation to any particular individual or group, efforts to determine the relative contributions of various actors to the legislative process are important if we are to have an indepth understanding of our polity.[1] That is, in order to comprehend why legislative policies have the form they do, we must "have some idea of the factors that converge to produce them and how they relate to each other."[2]

The evidence from this study indicates that the contributions of the Health Care Financing Administration (HCFA), and perhaps other administrative agencies, are underrated by many political theorists. Historically, as well as in much of contemporary literature, the President and the Congress have been given much of the "credit" in formulating legislation. Because of the dominating influence of these two forces, the contributions of the bureaucracy to the legislative process have been obscured.

The evidence from this study is clear that top policy makers in the White House and the Congress have become, in this age of program and administrative complexity, extensively dependent upon their bureaucratic subordinates for support in the legislative process. Of course, this implies that the bureaucratic subordinates have become extensively involved in legislative policy development. In the words of Chip Kahn, Minority Council, Subcommittee on Health, the House Committee on Ways and Means, "we could not do our jobs without the assistance of the bureaucracy. The legislature simply would not operate efficiently."

This study confirms James Anderson's assumption that one of the major reasons for this obscurity is the fact that the bureaucracy's involvement in the legislative process is frequently informal.[3] As a consequence, much of HCFA's activities and contributions in forming Medicare legislative initiatives are located beneath the surface of the formal legislative process. This subterranean system arose because our Constitution only provides the bureaucracy the ability to "advise" the President and the Congress on legislative matters. To this end, it offers support, recommendations, technical advice and professional assistance which can represent a significant portion of the substance of legislation.

Summary of Study Findings

The contributions of HCFA to the formulation of Medicare legislation support Max Weber's theory of bureaucracy. Evidence from the study's quantitative data collected from agency briefing books and Congressional documents and qualitative data from personal interviews, show a strong reliance on the agency by the Congress and the President in legislative development. Agency legislative resources typically take the form of (1) expertise about Medicare policy and operational capabilities; (2) scientific and analytical capabilities, and (3) the independent development of legislation as well as assisting in fashioning proposals initiated by the White House and the Congress.

Proponents of the Weberian theory maintain that these bureaucratic resources, based on administrative efficiency and technological knowledge, make agencies, such as HCFA, indispensable in the legislative process.[4] While it is clear that the agency does not possess a monopoly on these skills, virtually all of the study interviewees acknowledged in their dialogue and practice that HCFA is a vital contributor of these resources to the Medicare legislative process.

Let us now turn to some more specific contributions of the agency to the legislative process. The discussion will center around three areas: legislative formulation, research and analysis and integration. Although these areas overlap in some respects, each is of sufficient importance to warrant separate consideration.

Legislative Formulation

The overriding objective of this study is to empirically demonstrate that HCFA is a major source of ideas for inclusion in the President's and Congress' Medicare legislative agenda. We also traced the use of scientific research and identified ongoing patterns of agency interaction with the President and the Congress.

When we view the total spectrum of how the agency participates in the legislative process, we can conclude that HCFA is deeply entrenched in the development of legislative initiatives in both the Executive and Legislative Branches. HCFA staff typically becomes involved in the early stages of the legislative process because of their operational knowledge of programs and staffing resources. They become involved both formally and informally by providing inputs in the form of "technical assistance and recommendations" to the White House and Congress when legislation is being formulated. The study findings show that the extent of the agency contributions often go undetected because a significant portion of its involvement in the legislative process is informal—located beneath the surface of the formal enactment process.

For the most part, HCFA's formal legislative activities are tied to the formulation of the President's legislative package and the Congressional budget process. The evidence shows that HCFA developed legislative initiatives can constitute a substantial part of the President's Medicare legislative program. For example, fifty-one percent of the President's Medicare legislative recommendations to the Congress for Fiscal Year 1988 could be traced to HCFA's legislative recommendations. This percentage is thought to be considerably higher since this legislation also contains agency initiated proposals that were submitted to the White House in prior years that were not available to this research.

HCFA is also involved in the development of proposals that are generally not considered significant enough for inclusion in the President's formal legislative package. These proposals are submitted to the Congress separately in what is often referred to as the "cats and dogs" bill. Cats and dogs come from agency staff, often at very low levels, who have direct contact with Medicare fiscal intermediaries, hospitals and beneficiaries in the regular course of their jobs. These employees frequently discover administrative problems that are technical, low-cost and noncontroversial which require changes in the Medicare law.

HCFA's development of legislative initiatives for inclusion in the President's legislative packages and the "cats and dogs" bills reconfirm Steven Kelman's proposition that "government agencies often bring to the attention of the Congress and the White House problems that need examination and routinely provide specific proposals for dealing with problems."[5] This study expands upon Kelman's findings by identifying the mechanisms through which these legislative initiatives are developed and the process within the agency for their consideration.

The study findings show that HCFA's legislative activities within the Executive Branch and with the Congress are integrated into its daily activities. While the focus of the agency's legislative activities are concentrated in its Office of Legislation and Policy, involvement in the legislative process is dispersed throughout HCFA's five bureaus and twelve support offices. While some periods are more intense than others, the agency's interaction with key actors in the legislative process is continuous.

To be more precise, within the Executive Branch HCFA staff performs a full range of legislative services for the President including, investigating and defining problems, research, drafting and commenting on legislation, providing advice on alternative means of achieving goals and determining whether proposals are administratively feasible. Examples given throughout the study make clear that HCFA also serves as an independent initiator of legislative proposals as well as assisting in fashioning of White House initiatives.

Although it was not a primary focus of this study, its findings also demonstrate how HCFA is able to recognize its changing functional reality within the Executive Branch. This is particularly evident in how the agency adjusts the focus of its legislative initiatives. Since the inception of the Medicare program, the agency has operated under four different political administrations and successfully adjusted to different budgetary, political and social climates.

During the Johnson Administration in 1967, the origin of over

72 percent of the Medicare amendments enacted could be traced directly to the agency. There were few budgetary restraints and virtually no White House clearances under the then Democratic held White House and Democratic controlled Congress. Agency career staff reported that a very close and open relationship existed with the Congress in the development of legislative initiatives.

HCFA's sensitivity and ability to work within political constraints is particularly evident with recent Presidents who have come into office with a strong distrust toward the career civil service in the agency. In 1972 under a president who was highly distrustful of the motivations of the bureaucracy, nearly 90% of the Executive Branch provisions were included in the president's formal legislative package. Data from agency records and interviews indicate that the vast majority of these provisions originated in the Medicare bureau, HCFA's organizational predecessor.

This shows that the agency was able to work with a President who was distrustful of its motivations and to obtain approval of a high percentage of its legislative initiatives. This period also marked a downward trend in documented evidence of Congressional consultation with agency staff. However, both career and Congressional staff report that considerable Congressional consultation continued to take place at a subterranean level.

In more recent years under the Reagan Administration and more austere budgetary circumstances, the study demonstrates how agency career staff can work jointly with political appointees in the development of legislative initiatives. This was clearly demonstrated in the development of President Reagan's proposal to encourage greater competition in the health care sector as well as in the development of the Medicare Prospective Payment System.

The conclusion that is drawn from these examples is that the bureaucracy has the flexibility to adapt its role to changing political circumstances. HCFA's ability to shift in its legislative activities in accord with changes in budgetary, political and social needs appears to be more a reflection of its sense of social efficiency rather than to any measure of organizational or administrative processes.

This evidence reconfirms earlier findings by Aberback, Putnam and Rockman in their 1981 study of bureaucratic influence which indicates that the distinction between politicians who make legislative policy and bureaucrats who merely implement it does not realistically describe their roles in modern democracies. Rather, these authors find that both engage heavily in politics and each understands that the other plays a role in the legislative initiation process.[6]

Integration

An important byproduct of HCFA's relationship with the President and Congress is that it contributes enormously to the integration of the Executive and Legislative Branches of government. HCFA staff interacts with political appointees in the agency, the White House, Congressional committee staff and legislators on an ongoing basis.

The study shows that the principal contacts agency staff have with the Congress is through the cultivation of "good will" or through contacts with respect to gathering information about legislative proposals. Evidence presented in this study shows that HCFA is a primary source of information for legislative staff members. Reciprocally, agency staff frequently used their Congressional contacts to keep abreast of Congressional activities involving the Medicare program.

Frequently the most easily accessible and knowledgeable people with Congressional committees are the professional staff, who often serve as fiduciaries for members of Congress. It was also evident from the study findings that the more knowledgeable the committee staff member is on Medicare issues the more influential he/she is with the committee. This knowledge enables experienced Congressional staffer to influence the drift as well as the technical details of Medicare legislation. In the words of Wilbur Mills, former Chairman of the House Committee on Ways and Means, the staff's job is to "bring facts together for our use, to do the spade work for us." "This involves digging into the minds and moods of the congressmen who will actually do the voting.[7]

Through their frequent and ongoing contacts, committee staff and agency officials, working together on common problems, build up the kind of understanding which maximizes the effect of agency opinions upon committee decisions. Committee recommendations, in turn, are the primary determinants upon the content of laws passed by the Congress. It is these kind of relationships that provide much of the cement that binds the Legislative and Executive Branches together.[8]

These later relations provide a means of achieving an accommodation outside of what Emmette Redford has termed the "traditional model of democratic administration." As Redford notes, "In the American polity, administration is not a function solely of the Executive branch; it is a continuing function of both the Legislative and Executive Branches, exercised through parallel hierarchies in the two Branches interacting with each other." Within the web of political-administrative activity described by Redford, "decisions often are made in a consensus process which merges the Executive and Legislative Branches in a manner in which neither is in charge."[9]

While we observe that the techniques of agency interaction with the White House and the Congress are well established, these relationships have not been static. Available evidence suggests that the relationships between the agency, the White House and the Congress are dynamic. They have evolved markedly over the past 20 years due to changes in program life cycles, personal attributes of various administrators, political tensions resulting from divided party government and the development of independent staff and analytical resources in Congress.

Research and Policy Analysis

This study suggests that the use of formal social science research and legislative development is not an orderly process. Instead, the findings from formal research serves more to direct our mode thinking about public issues. That is, the findings from HCFA's formal research program appear to be targeted toward basic reforms of the health care system rather than being inextricably linked to the legislative process.

Despite success stories like the Medicare Prospective Payment System, concerns continue to exist among policy makers about the need to have a more orderly relationship leading from research to legislative development. These concerns will not be put to rest easily. In fact, these proponents often argue that the Medicare Prospective Payment System is a good example of what can be achieved if social scientists and political actors collaborate more closely.

Several reasons were found in the study which help to explain the lack of a direct relationship between research and the development of legislative initiatives. Chief among them is that the course of action indicated by the research may not be a viable political choice. In this respect, political, financing and timing considerations frequently preclude action predicated on research findings. Research findings are also begun for "symbolic reasons, or to delay making a decision."[10] It is apparent that in such cases there would be little or no relationship to legislative initiation.

There is also frequently an overlooked benefit to research which is that it is just as effective if it disproves a course of legislative action under congressional consideration. A case in point in how research findings were used to dissuade Congress from enacting a Medicare prospective payment system for hospital based physicians (i.e., radiologists, anesthesiologists and pathologists).

Research findings showed that while the Medicare Prospective Payment System for hospitals was a tremendous success, a similar system for physicians would have been a disaster. Agency research revealed that such a system for physicians would have been confusing to Medicare beneficiaries, caused considerable resentment from physicians and caused an administrative nightmare. Perhaps the main lesson to be gleaned from these findings is to recognize that in judging the value of research, our perspective must be broadened to include its impact on the overall thinking about public policies rather than limited to its direct impact on the development of legislation.

The bureaucracy appears to be a habitat in which experts find a wealth of opportunities to influence public policy. Don K. Price once wrote that "the development of public policy and the methods of its administration owed less in the long run to the process of conflict among political parties and social or economic pressure groups than to the more objective processes of research and discussion among professional groups."[11] The bureaucracy provides a "setting in which experts in and out of government can get together to work on policy problems." In most cases, this dialogue "occurs long before these problems become legislative issues or matters of public debate."[12]

While the evidence in this study does not fully support this position, it does suggest that this is valid for legislation with broad social and program impact. For these legislative initiatives, the relationship between research and legislative development appear to be more direct. The largest expansions or program reforms involving Medicare generally have a foundation in formal research. The Medicare Prospective Payment System for hospitals, coverage of hospice services and Medicare payment on the basis of diagnostic related groups for nursing home services were all legislative initiatives based upon formal research funded under HCFA contracts.

Looking at national health policy over the past fifteen years, Lynn Etheredge found evidence to support this perspective. Etheredge traced the significant influence of health services research in expanding government and private sector efforts to come to grips with health care financing and delivery and cost containment issues. She found that a number of major federal initiatives during this period—in health professions training, prepaid capitated delivery systems such as health maintenance organizations, utilization review, health planning—stemmed from health services research.[13]

While there appears to be no orderly process leading from formal research to legislation, it does seem clear that policy analysis permeates the activities of the legislative process. Policy analysis typically had the highest percentage of the five categories in the study involving research in the legislative process. Moreover, the greatest percentage of this analysis was linked to Executive Branch policy initiatives. In a separate research project, Edward C. Banfield found similar evidence of the growth of policy analysis in the Executive Branch. He also found that this growth has been paralleled by a comparable growth in policy analysis in the Legislative Branch.

Interviews with career, political and Congressional staffs validate that decision makers have a voracious appetite for information gathering and analysis. One interviewee inferred that HCFA's greatest contribution to the legislative process is "information." To this end, HCFA has dedicated an entire bureau, the Bureau of Data Management, solely to the function of gathering data, analyzing facts and figures and processing information. Since knowledge is often a source of power and influence in the legislative process, this is a tremendous resource for HCFA.

The agency has been a significant actor in investigating Medicare problems and revealing their complexities. This does not suggest, however, that the choices available to legislators have become any easier. But many legislators feel that the clarification of choices alone is a tremendous help. In this respect, the study findings suggest that the penetration of policy analysis in the legislative process has resulted in profound changes in the ethos of how decisions are made.

Implications for Our Concept of Government

The issues raised here bring into question the respective roles of "official policy makers" in the Executive and Legislative Branches "who possess legal authority to engage in the initiation of legislative policy"—that is, those policy makers who have direct constitutional authority to act on legislative initiatives.[14] Likewise, it brings a better perspective into the presumed autonomous relationship the Congress has with the bureaucracy.

Only by questioning the long standing assumptions about their respective roles in the legislative process can we fill the void in our understanding of the actual process. In this manner we can gain the necessary empirical evidence to discern clear cut patterns in the formulation of legislative initiatives.

If we take Nelson Polsby's advice and assume that "today's new legislative policies are likely to come about in ways similar to which policies were born in the past," then we can learn considerably from the study of past legislative initiatives. By identifying legislative patterns of behavior, these past legislative initiatives can serve as a "road map to the future."[15]

Such a road map might also assist those of us who want to initiate new legislative policies by preventing the misdirection of resources and pointing us toward paths that have led others to success. But the primary importance for those of us with a special interest in legislative policy formulation is that it is vital that we understand what goes on in the little black box labeled "legislative initiation." This is because in a democracy, it is essential that information be available on how government works, how decisions are made, what forces impact on policy making, and how opinions, especially those from outside the government, affect the formulations of legislative initiatives.

The implicit assumption here is that career civil servants are no less involved in determining the direction and character of Medicare legislative policy than politicians. Perhaps civil servants have a greater incentive to become involved in the legislative process since they will ultimately have responsibility for the details of its administration.

More fundamentally, this study fosters concern about our understanding of the nation's unwritten Constitution. Professor Richard J. Stillman characterizes it in this fashion: "How do we get citizens to wake up to the fact that an effective, honest administrative state plays a big part in maintaining the constitutional system today and so must be nurtured for sustaining our constitutional order for tomorrow."[16]

The recognition that career civil servants are no less involved in determining the direction and character of Medicare legislation has considerable implications for the concept our governmental system. It also highlights the need to empirically demonstrate their contributions and how civil servants participate in the legislative process in ways other than to faithfully implement the laws Congress and the President have enacted. Only through empirical investigations is it possible to show that they actively participate in the formulation of legislation, and that is a part of the function of public policy making, even that policy-making which can only be done constitutionally by the Congress and the President.

Notes

1. Ronald C. Moe and Steven C. Teel, "Congress as Policy-Maker: A Necessary Reappraisal," *Political Science Quarterly* (New York: Academy of Political Science), Vol. LXXXV, 1970, pp. 443–469.
2. Kenneth M. Dolbeare, *American Public Policy* (New York: McGraw-Hill Book Co. 1982) p. 9.
3. James E. Anderson, op. cit., pp. 34–35.
4. Gerth and Mills, op. cit.
5. Steven Kelman, *Making Public Policy* (New York: Basic Books, 1987), p. 898.
6. Joel D. Aberback, Robert D. Putnam and Bert A. Rockman, *Bureaucrats and Politicians In Western Democracies* (Cambridge, Mass.: Harvard University Press, 1981).
7. Arlen J. Large, "Help on the Hill," *Readings in American Government,* Editors: H. Malcolm McDonald, Wilfred D. Webb, Edward G. Lewis and William L. Strauss (New York: Thomas Y. Crowell Co., 1968) p. 309.

8. Some political scientists have referred to these features as "integrated policy making." For a more detailed discussion see Louis W. Koenig, *An Introduction To Public Policy* (New Jersey: Prentice-Hall, 1986).

9. Emmette S. Redford, op. cit.

10. Carolyn Ban and Elysa Ferrara, "Expanding the Concept for Utilization: Case Studies in the Organizational Uses of Evaluation," Unpublished paper, 1988.

11. Don K. Price, *Government and Science* (New York: University Press, 1954) pp. 99–133.

12. Francis E. Rourke, *Bureaucracy, Politics, and Public Policy,* Second edition, (Boston, Mass.: Little, Brown and Co., 1976) p. 132.

13. Lynn Etheredge, "Government and Health Care Costs: The Influence of Research Policy," *From Research Into Policy,* Editor: Marion Ein Lewin, (Washington, D.C.: American Enterprise Institute for Public Policy Research, 1986) pp. 7–20.

14. James E. Anderson, op. cit., pp. 34–35.

15. Nelson W. Polsby, *Political Innovation In America* (Connecticut: Yale University Press, 1984) p. 1.

16. Richard J. Stillman II, "The Future of the American Constitution and the Administrative State After the Bicentenial: Some Reflections," *Public Administration Review,* Vol. 48, No. 4, July/August, 1988, pp. 813–815.

Appendix 1

SEC.____. PAYMENTS TO HOSPITAL OUTPATIENT DEPARTMENTS OF RADIOLOGY.

(a) AMOUNTS PAYABLE.—Section 1833 of the Social Security Act (42 U.S.C. 13951) is amended—

(1) in subsection (a)(2)—

(A) by striking "and" in subparagraph (C),

(B) by adding "and" at the end of subparagraph (D), and

(C) by adding at the end thereof the following new subparagraph:

(E) with respect to radiology procedures performed by hospital outpatient departments of radiology, the amount determined under subsection (m);" and

(2) by adding at the end thereof the following new subsection:

"(m) (i) Subject to paragraph (2), the amount determined under this subsection is the amount determined under subsection (a)(2)(B).

"(2)(A) In order to receive payment under this part for a procedure described in subsection (a)(2)(E), each hospital shall with respect to a cost reporting period separately indicate in its cost report the number of times the procedure was performed with respect to an individual covered by the insurance program under this part and the aggregate cost of the procedure performed with respect to all such individuals.

(B) The aggregate amount of the payments to be made with respect to a hospital in a fiscal year under this part for a procedure described in subsection (a)(2)(E) shall not exceed the cost of:

(i) the total of the hospital's aggregate costs for such procedures (as required to be reported under-paragraph (1) for cost reporting periods in the fiscal year; and

(ii) the amount determined in accordance with subparagraph (C) multiplied by the total number of times the procedure was performed by the hospital (as required to be reported under paragraph (1)) during cost reporting periods in the fiscal year.

(C)(i) The amount determined in accordance with this subparagraph is the sum of—

"(I) the cost proportion (as defined in clause (ii)(I) of the amount determined by dividing the amount described in paragraph (B)(ii) and

"(II) the charge proportion (as defined in clause (ii)(II) of 62 percent of the prevailing charge of a fiscal year for the same procedure furnished in a physician's office.

"(ii) In this subparagraph:

"(I) the term 'cost proportion' means 65 per-percent in case of fiscal years 1988 and 1989 and 50 percent in the case of fiscal year 1990.

"(II) The term 'charge proportion' means 25 percent in the case of fiscal s 1988 and 1989 and 50 percent in the case of fiscal year 1990.

(b) CONFORMING AMENDMENT.—Section 1833(a)(2)(B) of such Act (42 U.S.C. 13951 (a)(2)(B) is amended in the matter preceding clause (i) by striking "(C) of (D)" and inserting in lieu thereof "(C), (D), or (E)".

(c) EFFECTIVE DATE.—The amendments made by sub-section (a) shall apply with respect to cost reporting periods beginning on or after January 1, 1988.

Appendix 2

PSEC *1066*. PAYMENTS TO HOSPITAL OUTPATIENT DEPARTMENTS FOR RADIOLOGY.

(a) AMOUNTS PAYABLE.—*Section 1833 of the Social Security Act (42 U.S.C. 13951) is amended—*

(1) in subsection (a)(2)—

(A) by striking "and" in subparagraph (C),

(B) by adding "and" at the end of subparagraph (D), and

(C) by adding at the end thereof the following new subparagraph:

"(E) with respect to—

"(i) outpatient hospital radiology services (including diagnostic and therapeutic radiology, nuclear medicine and CAT scan procedures, magnetic resonance imaging, and ultrasound and other imaging services), and

"(ii) effective for procedures performed on or after October 1, 1989, diagnostic procedures (as defined by the Secretary) described in section 1861(a)(3) (other than diagnostic X-ray tests and diagnostic laboratory tests),

the amount determined under subsection (n);", and

(2) by adding at the end, as previously amended, the following new subsection:

"(n)(I)(A) The aggregate amount of the payments to be made for all or part of a cost reporting period beginning on or after October 1, 1988 under this part for services described in subsection (aX2XE) shall be equal to the lesser of—

"(i) the amount determined with respect to such services under subsection (a)(2)(B), or

"(ii) the blend amount for radiology services and diagnostic procedures determined in accordance with subparagraph (B).

"(BXi) the blend amount for radiology services and diagnostic procedures for a cost reporting period is the sum of—

"(I) the cost proportion (as defined in clause (ii)) of the amount described in subparagraph (A)(i); and

"(II) the charge proportion (as defined in clause (ii)(II)) of 62 percent (for services described in subsection (a)(2)(E)(i)), or (for procedures described in subsection (a)(2)(E)(ii)), 42 percent or such other percent established by the Secretary (or carriers acting pursuant to guidelines issued by the Secretary) based on prevailing charges established with actual charge data, of 80 percent of the prevailing charge for participating physicians for the same services as if they were furnished in a physician's office in the same locality as determined under section 1842(b).

"(ii) In this subparagraph:

"(I) The term 'cost proportion' means 65 percent for all or any part of cost reporting periods which occur in fiscal year 1989 and 50 percent for other cost reporting periods.

"(II) The term 'charge proportion' means 35 percent for all or any parts of cost reporting periods which occur in fiscal year 1989 and 50 percent for other cost reporting periods".

(b) CONFORMING AMENDCMENT.—*Section 1833(a)(2)(B) of such Act (42 U.S.C. 13951(a)(2)(B)) is amended in the matter preceding clause (i) by striking "(C) or (D)" and inserting "(C), (D), or (E)".*

(c) EFFECTIVE DATE.—*The amendments made by subsection (a) shall apply with respect to outpatient hospital radiology services furnished on or after October 1, 1988, and other diagnostic procedures performed on or after October 1, 1989.*

Index

Biographical Sketch

Chester A. Robinson, D.P.A., is Chief of the Evaluation Branch, Bureau of Health Resources Development, Health Resources and Services Administration (HRSA). He has also served as Chief of the Legislative, Regulatory and Policy Branch in HRSA.

He was with the Health Care Financing Administration for 17 years in a variety of positions involving legislation and policy development, research on long term care issues, and Medicare program operations. Much of the information used in this book was collected during this period.

Dr. Robinson received his doctorate degree in Public Administration from George Mason University in 1989, Master of Policy Sciences from the University of Maryland in 1980, Master of Liberal Arts from Johns Hopkins University in 1975 and a Bachelor of Arts from Grambling State University in 1971. His other research interests include assessing health care delivery for acquired immunodeficiency syndrome (AIDS) patients, organ transplantation and the impact of federal financing on the construction of health care facilities.